THEATRE MODELS

---— ❋ ---—

IN PAPER AND CARD

£2

THEATRE MODELS

IN PAPER AND CARD

ROBERT BURGESS

GUILD OF MASTER CRAFTSMAN PUBLICATIONS LTD

First published 1999 by
Guild of Master Craftsman Publications Ltd,
166 High Street, Lewes,
East Sussex, BN7 1XU

© Robert Burgess 1999

ISBN 1 86108 110 3

Photographs of theatres and cover photograph by Zul Mukhida
Step-by-step photographs by Mark Haynes-Kershaw
Line drawings and templates by Robert Burgess
Photograph on page 20 by Stephen Hepworth

I am indebted to the publishers of the following books for permission to use images from their publications: Gillon, Edmund, **Picture Sourcebook for Collage and Decoupage**, Dover; Lehner, Ernst, **Symbols, Signs and Signets**, Dover; **Architecture Drawings**, Pepin Press; **Graphic Ornaments**, Pepin Press; **Ornamental Design**, Pepin Press; Harthan, John, **The History of the Illustrated Book**, Thames & Hudson, page 164. Bernardo Castello, Rodomonte wreaks havoc in a city square, canto 17, Lodovic Anosto, Orlando Furioso, Venice. Stefano Orlandini, 1730 (Filosi)
The author also wishes to thank the Theatre Institute, Amsterdam, for unlimited access to the Guido Van Deth collection of toy theatre books.

The photographs on page 7 and 8 were reproduced with the kind permission of Pollock's Toy Theatre Museum.

Designed by Mind's Eye Design, Lewes.
Cover designed by Wheelhouse Design.
Typefaces: New Baskerville and Trajan.

Colour origination by Viscan Graphics (Singapore)
Printed and bound by Kyodo Printing (Singapore) under the supervision of MRM Graphics, Winslow, Buckinghamshire, UK

CONTENTS

FOREWORD

Toy theatre, the darling of the Victorian drawing room, is making remarkable progress toward becoming a genuinely contemporary medium. It has always been a great mode of artistic expression, not only because it can be so elegant in its miniature recreation of grand drama and opera, but because it is so accessible. Anyone can do it with a least amount of expense!

In *Theatre Models in Paper and Card*, Robert Burgess gives meticulous directions on how you can make your very own splendid little twentieth-century version of a Victorian model theatre. What is truly thrilling is that the transition is made without sacrificing either the whimsy or style for which this theatre form is so well known.

This book is a substantial contribution to the model theatre scene; I am proud to have been invited to write a few words about this book and its author. We hope readers will enjoy making the designs contained in this book and go on to make some original designs of their own.

Gigi Sandberg, Secretary, Puppeteers of America

INTRODUCTION

This book was born out of my fascination with toy theatre. My passion for the subject began when I was just a small child, and has stayed with me throughout the years. I have been inspired, partly by my work as a designer and illustrator, to adapt and stylize the toy theatre. I hope I have updated and modernized toy theatre design while staying true to the essence of the original idea, but I apologize to purists in advance!

One Christmas Eve when I was seven, Santa Claus, disguised as my father, delivered a wonderful and breathtaking present – a professionally constructed theatre with a stage so big I could walk across it. It almost filled our sitting room. How my parents had managed to keep it from my prying eyes I still cannot fathom to this day. The theatre was complete with a hand-painted proscenium arch, gilded and ornate in the baroque style, red velvet and gold-fringed curtains on a real curtain track with weighted pull cords, wings, scenery, props for the pantomime, Cinderella, and a complete cast of puppets. To top it all, my theatre had footlights and spotlights with dimmer controls and special effects, all run by a simple secondhand car battery, neatly disguised in an alcove at the side of the stage. A world of wonder and miracle opened up before my very eyes.

Many of the projects in this book are inspired by the original toy theatres of the nineteenth century. The Victorian Theatre Royale is the most similar to the original designs of this period. The Punch and Judy Booth and the Bali Shadow Theatre have an attraction and a mystery of their own, and I am sure you will agree that they deserve a place in any book about contemporary toy theatre design.

CHAPTER ONE

HOW TO
USE THIS BOOK

This book offers a comprehensive guide to making toy theatres, but I hope you will find much more than just this within these pages. My aim is to provide inspiration and to stimulate interest in the imaginative possibilities of toy theatre design and construction. Toy theatres are a surprisingly undervalued art form. They are mainly thought of as children's toys, yet the potential they offer for decorative design is enormous.

THE PROJECTS

Included within these pages are 10 simple projects, all clearly illustrated with step-by-step photographs. Different styles and decorating schemes are covered in each project – from the atmospheric Winter Wonderland, to the traditional Punch and Judy Booth, inspired by childhood seaside memories, via the exotic and mysterious Bali Shadow Theatre.

When you first browse through this book you may think that an abundance of skills, tools and technical expertise will be needed to complete any of the projects. This is not the case. The projects are constructed using a range of simple craft techniques. All the basic skills you will need are explained in detail in Chapter Six (see page 21). This book has been carefully designed so that you can work steadily through it from cover to cover or, if you are a more advanced and accomplished craftsperson, pick out the projects which appeal to you most.

EQUIPMENT AND MATERIALS

Detailed advice is given on the materials and equipment needed for each project at the beginning of the relevant chapter. Chapters Four and Five suggest a basic kit of tools and outline the types of material you will need (see pages 12 and 18). You may find you already have most of the basic tools around your home. The materials used in the projects are readily available at your local art and craft shop, or you can order by mail from the suppliers indicated at the back of the book (see page 147).

THE PLAYERS

Traditionally, the characters or figures in toy theatre are manipulated by wires, rods or card strips which are pushed through slits in the side or back of the theatre. For some of the theatres in this book it will be necessary to construct your own cast of players to complete the project, especially if your finished creation is intended for a child. Ideas for characters can be found in a number of places, from magazines to comics, children's books to new or used greetings cards. For a real touch of originality, why not draw and colour the characters yourself?

WHERE NEXT?

Colour and imagery are essential ingredients of the toy theatre. The imaginative way in which these elements are applied to a basic theatre design can result in any number of fantastic creations. You can adapt and develop the designs and illustrations throughout this book for your own projects. Learning to apply your newly-acquired skills will be an enjoyable experience, leading to beautiful theatres for your own and others' enjoyment.

If you turn to the further reading section at the end of this book (see page 149), I have listed a handful of wonderful books that will help you to expand your interest in, and knowledge of, beautiful craft techniques and toy theatres.

Why not set yourself a brief to design and create a theatre for a special family occasion or anniversary? Let your favourite artist, author or building inspire you. Remember that nothing is set in stone, adapt ideas to suit yourself and the supplies and materials you have at hand.

CHAPTER TWO

A BRIEF HISTORY
OF THE TOY THEATRE,
PEEPSHOWS AND PUPPETRY

It would be impossible to offer a complete history of toy theatre within this chapter. The subject is so vast that I hope you will forgive me if I just skim the surface, putting the fascinating crafts of toy theatre, peepshows and world puppetry into historical context. These great traditions have influenced and inspired me to create the projects included in this book.

PEEPSHOWS

An early predecessor of the toy theatre was the peepshow – a fascinating but simple idea. A theatrical scene is viewed through a tiny aperture pierced in the end of a small box. Holes are cut in the top of the box and covered in coloured tissue paper to allow a mysterious and intriguing light to filter through. The scenery is arranged in layers, reaching back from the peephole to the far end of the box. The characters are attached to strips of

A simple peepshow

4

A concertina-fold theatre

card, which extend from the sides of the box through small slits, so they can be pulled on and off stage (see left).

From the early nineteenth century, a variation of the peepshow took a concertina or folding form. This inspired my Folding Theatre in a Box, a modern version of the theatre shown here (see page 39). The concertina theatre is a simple construction made up of a backdrop with scenery sheets arranged in layers in front of it. Concertina strips of paper, linen or thin card are threaded through the scenery sheets and attached to the front and back of the theatre. The frontispiece can either become a proscenium arch or a peephole.

The concertina strips allow the theatre to be pulled out for viewing and packed away neatly. Each sheet of scenery has part of the middle section cut away, allowing the viewer to see through to the next layer. When the theatre is extended, this creates a convincing three-dimensional effect, a technique which is used in several of the projects in this book (see page 26).

There have been many variations using the basic techniques of the peepshow over the years, including elaborate and complicated Victorian Christmas cards, such as Nativity scenes where the figures can be manipulated by strips sliding through slits in the sides or base. Modern day pop-up cards have their origins in the humble peepshow, which inspired my Pop-up Theatre Greetings Card (see page 45).

THE BEGINNINGS OF TOY THEATRE

The origins of toy theatre are unclear, although William West is sometimes credited with its invention. He owned a shop near Covent Garden which sold a variety of things, including children's toys. In 1811 he started printing and selling sheets of characters from a popular pantomime of the time. The sheets sold extremely well. He was soon making complete toy theatres with a proscenium arch, stage and scenery. Other toy theatre publishers sprang up as the popularity of toy theatre spread.

West, and other publishers, sent out artists to draw real-life theatre productions of the day. The theatre framework, the proscenium arch and pediment decoration, was often copied from the architecture of real theatres. The character puppets were generally designed to be pushed onto the stage with wires. Each character would be drawn in a variety of attitudes for dramatic effect. Toy theatre publishers even provided copies of tickets so children could charge for their performances.

West printed his theatres on high quality paper, but as toy theatre gained in popularity other publishers sought to cut costs. By the 1830s it was common to print toy theatre sheets on cheaper paper. You may have heard of the phrase 'penny plain, twopence coloured'. This refers to the sheets of the proscenium arch, characters and scenery, which were once sold uncoloured for one penny or hand-coloured for twopence. The colouring of the sheets was usually bright and garish.

Over 300 plays were produced in toy theatre form in England in the nineteenth century. During this era toy theatre was also popular across Europe, especially in Denmark, Germany and Austria. Although toy theatres continued to be produced until the beginning of the twentieth century, their heyday came during the mid-nineteenth century.

SHADOW THEATRE

Cultures throughout the world have their own unique traditions of puppet theatre. Shadow theatre is still a significant part of culture and society in many countries. The exotic and mysterious art of shadow theatre is achieved by projecting images onto a taut linen or parchment screen which is illuminated from behind by a light. The shadow artist manipulates puppets between the light and the screen. The type of figure used depends on the country concerned. I have included a project which is based on Indonesian shadow theatre (see page 89).

The ancient Indonesian art of shadow play, or 'wayang kulit', is overseen by the Dalang, who is a master of his craft. Not only does he narrate the story, but he manipulates all the characters, interprets and performs voices for each of them. He is expected to produce sound effects, speech and movement. As if this was not enough, he also sings and directs the music. The Dalang are highly respected expert craftsmen and create all of their own characters. It is traditional to pass the craft down to the younger members of the family.

Similar shadow theatre traditions also survive in other parts of the world including China and Japan, Turkey and Greece, although in Turkey and Greece their popularity is in decline in recent years.

A scene from Red Riding Hood, Webb theatre, c1850

PUNCH AND JUDY

And finally a word about Punch and his dutiful wife Judy, undeniably our most popular national puppet. Again, sadly, Punch and Judy shows are declining in number. It seems that they are not compatible with the phenomenon of 'political correctness'. Perhaps, like the toy theatre of the nineteenth century, Punch and his dear wife Judy will experience a revival in the not too distant future? Until that time I will pay homage to that loveable couple by dedicating the Punch and Judy project (see page 75) to them and their loyal followers.

A scene from Dick Whittington, Pollock's Neptune theatre, c1850

TOY THEATRE TODAY

There has recently been a revival in interest in the toy theatre. Pollock's Toy Theatre Museum in London now produces toy theatres using original Victorian designs. The museum takes its name from Benjamin Pollock, one of the last toy theatre publishers. He died in 1937, but his stock was bought up by interested parties and the tradition of toy theatre publishing continues at Pollock's Museum to this day. The museum also houses an impressive collection of toy theatres and other antique toys and is well worth a visit, see page 147 for its address.

PART I

THE BASICS

CHAPTER THREE

BUILDING BLOCKS
OF THE TOY THEATRE

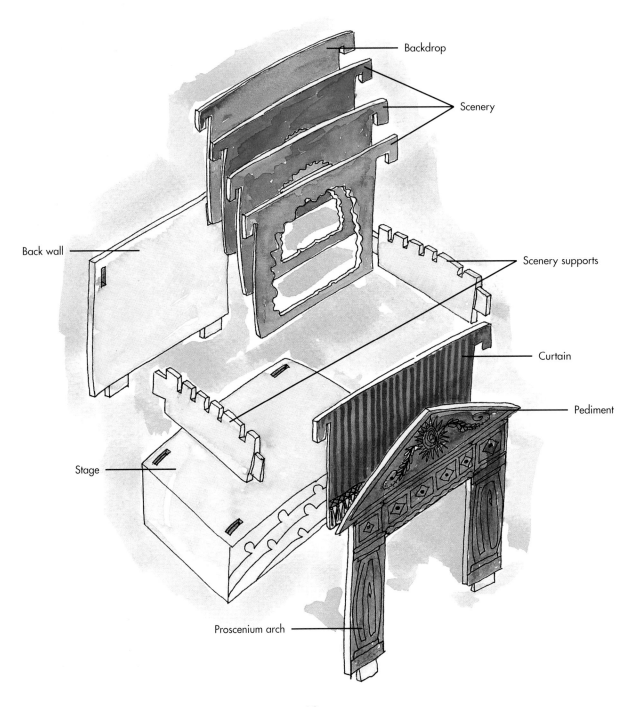

Backdrop

Scenery

Back wall

Scenery supports

Curtain

Pediment

Stage

Proscenium arch

STAGE

The stage is one of the most important parts of a theatre. It is the foundation on which the whole theatre is constructed. In the earliest toy theatres, the stage was made from wood and covered with cardboard. An orchestra strip, showing the instrumentalists who accompany the performance in the orchestra pit, is often attached to the front of the stage, as it is here.

PROSCENIUM ARCH

The proscenium arch is the most decorative part of the theatre framework. The original toy theatres of the nineteenth century were often miniature copies of the real theatres of the day. Proscenium arch decoration can range from the stark and minimalist, to the fun and frolics of baroque and rococo eccentricity. The arch separates the audience from stage and frames the set, drawing the viewer's eye to the magical scene beyond.

PEDIMENT

The proscenium arch can be topped with a decorative pediment.

BACKDROP

The backdrop scene can either be fixed to the back wall of the theatre, or take the form of a sheet hung from the scenery supports, just in front of the back wall. It often features a distant view or a glimpse of sky.

BACK WALL

The scenery supports are attached to the back wall of the theatre.

SCENERY

This brings the theatre alive ready for the players to take their place on stage. Scenery drops, or sheets, are hung from the scenery supports. The sheets are painted and have parts cut away, allowing the audience to see through to the next layer. Alternatively, scenery wings can be placed either side of the stage.

Scenery is designed to give the illusion of depth and create atmosphere. Several layers of scenery artfully decorated and arranged can transform the stage into a three-dimensional space.

SCENERY SUPPORTS

Scenery supports are generally attached between the back wall and proscenium arch of the theatre. They create a simple support on which scenery can be hung. They also help to strengthen the construction of the theatre framework.

CURTAINS

Curtain designs can range from simple red velvet swathes with heavy fringing and ropes and tassels, to stark, plain sheets.

CHAPTER FOUR

TOOLS AND EQUIPMENT

MARKING, DRAWING AND CUTTING EQUIPMENT

Circle cutter

A circle cutter looks a little like a compass, but has a blade instead of a slot for a pencil. The basic model is usually calibrated for cutting circles from ⅜in to 6in (10mm to 152mm) in diameter. It is possible to cut a circle with a scalpel, or craft knife, but the result is not as professional as when a circle cutter is used. You will only need the most basic model of circle cutter for the projects in this book. For instance, a circle cutter will be useful when cutting the portfolio box fastener for the Folding Theatre in a Box.

Marking and cutting equipment

Cutting mats

A cutting mat will help to avoid accidental furniture damage. They also extend the life of your scalpel blade. Cutting mats are available in a vast array of sizes. An A3 mat is a good size to use initially, although you can get by with an A4 one. Most cutting mats are self healing, which means that any cuts in the mat reseal themselves. When cutting larger pieces of card or paper, a thick pile of old newspaper will do the job, but you will need to replace the newspapers regularly.

Metal rules

A metal rule is essential for cutting straight lines using a scalpel or craft knife. For measuring, a plastic or wood ruler will do, but do not cut against these as the blade will render them useless in a short time.

Scalpel and blades or craft knife

I prefer using a scalpel for cutting detailed shapes, although a good craft knife with a snap-off blade will suffice. Remember to follow basic safety rules (see page 21).

Scissors

Scissors are useful for cutting larger items, and cutting roughly around small images before using the scalpel for detailed cutting.

Technical drawing pens

You don't need to buy an expensive set of technical drawing pens, e.g. Rotring or Faber Castell, for the projects in this book. There are some good, cheap, non-refillable versions on the market. Drawing pens are good for adding an outline to finished work. They are classified by the thickness of line they draw. Useful line widths are 0.25 for fine lines, and 0.5 for heavy outlining.

Pencils

I find the HB pencil the most adaptable type of pencil, as it is neither too hard nor too soft. An HB pencil is useful for tracing and transferring images because it leaves the right amount of graphite residue on the tracing paper. You can use other grades of pencil for tracing, but remember that F pencils will need more pressure to make a mark and may leave a non-removable groove, especially on watercolour and paper. Heavier pencils, such as B to 6B pencils, can be messy to use and leave a heavy residue. Choose a pencil which suits your purpose and which you feel comfortable using.

Chinagraph pencils

A chinagraph pencil is useful for marking shiny surfaces, like glass and plastic. These pencils come in a range of colours, but I prefer to use blue and white. I use chinagraph pencils for drawing image outlines onto lino and scraperboard (scratchboard) before they are cut or scraped with the appropriate tools. Chinagraph pencils can also be used to draw on acetate.

Clamps

Simple, cheap C clamps help to hold sheets of glued card together while the glue is drying. Bulldog clips can serve the same purpose.

Compass

A pair of compasses will draw accurate circles. For larger circles a drawing pin fastened to a piece of string, with a pencil tied to one end, is just as effective. I have also been known to use a dinner plate as a template.

Dressmakers' pins

Like clamps, pins can be used to hold pieces in place during gluing. A few pins strategically placed in your paper or card will hold things together until the glue is dry. Pins are particularly useful for holding pieces of card or paper in place over a curved surface.

Rivets and rivet tools

It is worth investing in a rivet tool and rivets. They are handy to have in your kit. Simple eyelet rivets, which join two pieces of card together, are both useful and decorative. I used a simple eyelet rivet for attaching circular fastener to the Folding Theatre in a Box portfolio case (see page 43). There are various types and sizes of rivets on the market. They are available in silver, gold and other colours.

COLOURING EQUIPMENT

Colouring pencils

There is a wide range of colouring pencils available from art and craft shops. Colouring pencils can be used as an alternative to other colouring mediums, such as paint. Watercolour pencils create an effect very much like watercolour paint, and they are simple to use. Apply a light coat of colour with the pencil, then wash over with a brush dipped in water. The colour will dissolve, leaving you with a beautiful watercolour effect.

Colouring equipment

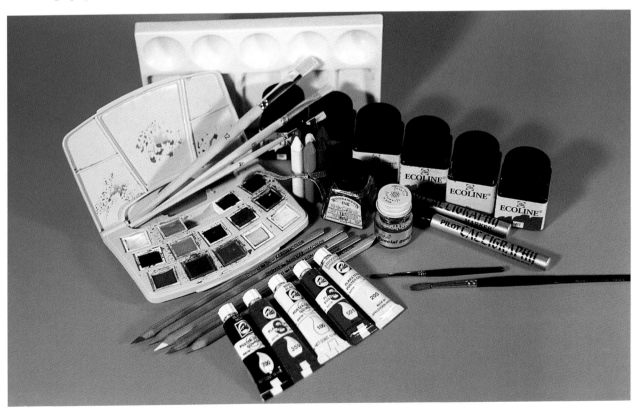

Gouache

Gouache is a water soluble opaque paint. Black and white paints, and a simple set of three colours – lemon yellow, light blue and Tyrian purple – can be mixed to achieve a fantastic spectrum of colours. Opaque white gouache can be used alongside watercolours for special effects. For instance, when white gouache is 'splattered', from an old toothbrush or stencil brush, over a deep blue watercolour background, an atmospheric starry night effect is created.

Watercolour paint

Watercolours can be transparent when used effectively, allowing the white of the watercolour paper to show through. For the best results, use a lot of water with the paint, and treat yourself to a good sable brush. Watercolour paints hold water well and are lovely to use. A limited palette of yellow, blue, red and Payne's Gray can create good results for a beginner. Poster paint is a type of watercolour paint and can be used to create the same effects.

Drawing ink

I like to keep pots of gold, silver and Indian ink in my toolbox. Inks, applied with a traditional drawing pen and nib, are excellent for adding finishing touches to coloured images. For instance, crosshatching with black ink can emphasize shadows. Metallic inks can be used to add detail and decoration to curtains and proscenium arches.

Watercolour inks

These inks are ready mixed and available in some stunning colours. They can be mixed with water to achieve different intensities of shade. The advantage of watercolour inks is that they create strong colours and are easy to use.

Spray paints

Sometimes spray paint is the ideal solution to a colouring job. I use spray paints for larger surfaces. They also work well when used for stencilling. A light spray of gold and silver, over a black and white photocopied image, can give a subtle 'knocked back' effect, whereby the photocopied image just shows through the paint. Do not forget to keep a window open, or ensure you have adequate ventilation, when using spray paints. Cover any surfaces before you start and always wear a mask.

Gilding and transfer metal leaf

There are several different types of metal leaf, including Dutch metal leaf, a cheaper yet effective alternative to real gold leaf and aluminium leaf. Dutch metal leaf is used in the projects which follow. For details of how to use metallic leafing, see page 28.

Wax crayons

Crayons can be used effectively underneath watercolour paints or inks to achieve texture and interest. The wax repels the water and can create interesting and sometimes unexpected effects. Try drawing some clouds on watercolour paper using a white crayon or candle, then cover the paper with a blue watercolour wash.

Paintbrushes

Synthetic decorating paintbrushes are suitable for colourwashing and applying glue to larger areas. A smaller synthetic brush will be useful for applying glue to smaller pieces of card and paper. I also would recommend investing in three round brushes for watercolour painting in sizes 1, 5 and 13. Sable brushes are generally high quality, but the synthetic brushes made today are also very good.

Paint rollers and tray

Small paint rollers are useful for applying colour to larger areas. You will find these in hardware stores and decorating outlets.

ADHESIVES

Two-part epoxy glue

The best known brand name for this type of glue is Araldite Rapid. Two-part epoxy glue is very strong, and can be used when other glues are not effective. It is particularly useful for attaching heavier decorative objects. I tend to use this type of glue at the finishing and decorative stages of making a theatre. For instance, I used it to attach the picture hanger at the back of the Three-Dimensional Picture Theatre.

Adhesives and adhesive tapes

Two-part epoxy glue comes in two tubes, equal parts of each tube need to be blended together with cocktail stick or matchstick before applying. You may need to support the glued pieces for a couple of hours, until the glue is completely dry. Any excess glue needs to be wiped away directly after application, otherwise it will show when dry.

Stick glues

Stick glue is a useful glue to have in your craft kit. Pritt Stick is one of the most generally known brands of stick glue. They are not ideal for every job, but they are quick, clean and easy to apply. I use it to stick a number of small images on to an A4 or A3 sheet of paper to make a master sheet, ready for photocopying. Stick glue is also useful for attaching edges and corners which become unstuck. The disadvantage of this type of glue is that it tends to cause wrinkles when applied to larger areas.

PVA

PVA (polyvinyl acetate) is by far the most popular and versatile glue in the art and craft world. It is also known as white glue or woodworkers' glue. It can be used as an adhesive or as a binding agent to mix with other mediums, such as colour pigments or sand and sawdust to give texture. It can also be used as a varnish and sealant (when diluted with water on a one part glue to three parts water basis). It is widely available in art and craft outlets and hardware shops.

Silicone rubber

Silicone rubber, also known as three-dimensional glue, is used extensively for three-dimensional decoupage. It is available in art and craft outlets. A small ball of glue can be squeezed from the tube and removed with a matchstick or cocktail stick. I use a few small balls of silicone rubber to attach an image so that it is slightly raised from its background.

Spray glue

Spray glues are expensive, but are clean and easy to use. Spray mount does not attach things permanently straight away, allowing pieces to be lifted and repositioned. I find spray mount becomes more permanent with age. Display mount is permanent from the moment it is applied. It is useful for small, quick jobs. It forms an extremely smooth surface and does not cause wrinkles. When using spray glues ensure you have a well-ventilated area and use a mask.

Adhesive tapes

Single-sided adhesive tape can provide support when two pieces of card are being glued together, i.e. making the stage section of Theatre Grande (page 95). Where it will not be seen, the adhesive tape can be left attached for extra support.

Double-sided adhesive tape provides instant contact between two surfaces. It is quick, clean and suitable for small fiddly jobs.

Masking tape can be used to protect areas from being painted or sprayed. It is also useful for attaching tracing paper to images, to stop them from moving, or for holding pieces of card together until the glue is dry. Unlike single-sided adhesive tape, masking tape can be peeled off without damaging the paper or card it has been attached to. I find the 'low tack' type works best.

CHAPTER FIVE

MATERIALS

BROWN WRAPPING PAPER

Brown wrapping paper is readily available from a variety of outlets. It is a very versatile paper. I use it for covering cardboard, providing an adequate surface for paint and other decorative effects. Wrapping paper similar to the basic brown-coloured paper is available in silver and gold.

METALLIC FOIL PAPER

Most foil papers consist of a metallic surface with a paper backing. Foil-covered cardboard is available for heavier work. Metallic foil paper can be used for decorative finishes and for creating atmospheric effects such as stars and moons.

HANDMADE PAPERS

There are some beautiful handmade papers available. They can sometimes be expensive, so are best used occasionally to give a really special finish.

TISSUE PAPER

These range from the basic tissue papers, generally used for wrapping, to the more expensive 'silk' tissues, which are made from shreds of fabric. Cheaper tissue paper can provide a beautiful textured finish if it is slightly crumpled, flattened and glued to a flat surface. Once smoothed the paper will form delicate veins. The paper can then be varnished with a thin coat of PVA, mixed with water, to protect the surface.

PARCHMENT

Parchment is a translucent but strong paper. I used it for the screen on the Bali Shadow Theatre (page 89). There are suitable, and cheaper, alternatives to parchment, such as tracing paper, or two or three sheets of white tissue paper.

WATERCOLOUR PAPER

Watercolour papers are available in an array of weights and textures. As its name implies, watercolour paper provides the best surface for watercolour paints.

TRACING PAPERS

Tracing paper is available in various weights, but for simple image transfer a light to medium-weight paper will suffice. Tracing paper is translucent, which enables an image to be seen through its surface, making it easy to copy with.

BOX CARD

Box card is a form of cardboard. It is usually grey in colour and is used extensively in the packaging industry. I have used the heavier types of card, 600gsm, 800gsm and 1400gsm, for the projects in this book because they do not bend easily.

BRISTOL BOARD

Bristol board is available in an array of weights and thickness. The light and medium-weight card is useful for backing photocopied paper images, especially when part of the image is going to be cut away to create a three-dimensional decoupage effect.

CORRUGATED CARD

Most large boxes are constructed from corrugated card. I have used corrugated card to make the framework of the larger theatres, e.g. Theatre Grande. Two or more sheets of corrugated card can be glued together from two, three or even four-ply cardboard. This can then be used to produce strong and hardwearing theatre parts, such as scenery supports. When covered with paper, corrugated card almost resembles wood, although it is much lighter.

Most of the corrugated card that I have used in many of the projects is recycled! I do a weekly tour of my local shops and ask for any old cardboard boxes and cartons going spare. Most shops are usually glad to get them off the premises.

MICRO-CORRUGATED CARD

Micro-corrugated card is much finer than ordinary corrugated card. It is usually available in black and brown and is useful for more delicate and intricately-cut theatre parts. It also scores and folds well, making it suitable for boxes and containers.

WAVY-CORRUGATED CARD

Wavy-corrugated card is a decorative card. It is also available in zigzag shapes.

Scraperboard (scratchboard)

This illustrative technique has been with us for a long time, and now seems to be making a revival. Scraperboard is a heavy card coated with a layer of white china clay and finished with a surface of black ink. The black surface created by the ink is scratched away, using a set of special tools, to reveal the white of the clay underneath. The contrast between the white and black produce a striking image that reproduces particularly well on the photocopier.

Scraperboard is also available without the surface of black ink, to enable you to apply a surface to the white chalk coating in a colour and a medium of your choice.

Photocopy paper

The usual weight of paper used in photocopiers is between 80gsm and 100gsm. Whatever your local copy shop uses for standard black and white copying will be suitable for the projects in this book. Standard British paper sizes are:
- A4 11¾in x 8¼in (298mm x 210mm),
- A3 16½in x 11¾in (419mm x 295mm).

The closest U.S. equivalents are:
- 11in x 8½in (279mm x 216mm) for A4,
- 17in x 11in (432mm x 279mm) for A3.

Textured, heavy and recycled papers and the rougher handmade papers, any papers with loose fibres, leaves, flowers or shavings will not work well in photocopiers. If you are not sure whether the paper you want to use is suitable, ask the experts in the copy shop. As a rule of thumb, smooth finishes give a much better result.

Decorative extras

Decorative finishing touches can be achieved with a number of simple shapes and accessories. Metallic stars, moons and other motifs are readily available in art and craft shops. Start a collection of ribbons, foil motifs and glitter, they will all come in useful one day.

A range of decorative papers, cards and tissue papers

CHAPTER SIX

TECHNIQUES

CUTTING

A self-healing cutting mat and a scalpel are the best cutting tools, although a good pair of sharp-pointed scissors will suffice on occasion. A scalpel is a necessity for precise three-dimensional decoupage. For thicker, inflexible card I would recommend using a craft knife.

Of course, extra care must be taken when using scalpels and craft knives. Here are a few safety tips:
• always cut away from your hand and use a metal rule,
• remember to change your blades frequently when using scalpels and craft knives,
• a blunt blade does not do the job well, and the extra pressure needed when using an old blade can cause slipping or snapping, resulting in injury.

GLUING

You will find a range of adhesives described and illustrated on page 16. I have not suggested specific adhesives for each project. This is because I believe we all have a favourite glue or tape which we prefer to use for particular things.

I can recommend petroleum-based glues such as UHU or Bostik Clear for everyday use. Good results can also be obtained with white adhesives such as Copydex or PVA. Bookbinders' glue is fantastic for gluing larger areas. Of course, spray mount or display mount are easy to use and controllable, if somewhat expensive.

Remember apply all glue sparingly – too much can ruin the job in hand.

SCORING

You will find it necessary, in some of the projects, to crease and fold the paper or card, creating a crisp and accurate finish. To achieve a good result the paper or card must be scored first, so that it folds cleanly and in the right place. Your aim is to compress the fibres of the paper or card so that it will fold and bend easily, but not to cut right through. A little practice will make perfect.

There are various ways of scoring paper and card. Bookbinders use a bone scorer; a tool made specially for scoring with. A good alternative to this is to wrap some masking tape around one end of a jumbo paperclip to make a grip. The other rounded end of the clip is perfect for scoring with. As a last resort, an old ballpoint pen that has run out of ink will also do the job.

PHOTOCOPYING

Photocopied decorative images ready to be cut out

Simple black and white copies are an important part of the projects contained in this book. Photocopiers can be used to enlarge or reduce images at the touch of a button, saving a lot of time and painstaking calculations.

Most of the the decorative images need to be enlarged by 200%, which is the equivalent of enlarging from A5 size to A3 size. There is a section at the beginning of each project which will refer you to the pages you need to photocopy.

In some cases, you may need to enlarge images 400% to create A3 sheets to cover theatre parts with, or, in the case of the Bali Shadow Theatre, to copy the decoration of the proscenium arch. Don't worry if the photocopier you are using only enlarges by 200%, just photocopy the image once at 200% then photocopy this enlarged image by 200% to make a 400% enlargement. When enlarging images like this you may need to spend some time positioning the image on the photocopy glass to ensure that the resulting photocopy fits easily onto the page.

Black and white photocopiers can be found in copy shops, libraries and sometimes even newsagents. Although the photocopy requirements of this book are straightforward, I have found from experience that it is worth building up a friendly relationship with your photocopy operator – ask their advice and, most of all, be patient during busy periods. The good news is that copy shops are springing up everywhere. Many places will allow you to operate the photocopier yourself, so you can experiment, using the machine at your own speed.

TRACING AND TRANSFERRING IMAGES

When the paper which you want to transfer images onto is not photocopy friendly, you can trace the image using a traditional technique.

The project you see demonstrated here is the Pop-up Theatre Greetings Card (see page 45). The images supplied on pages 110–111 need to be transferred onto watercolour paper which cannot go through a photocopier.

1 Take a photocopy of the image. Attach a piece of tracing paper to the surface of the photocopied image, securing it in place with masking tape to prevent it from slipping. Carefully draw over the image on the tracing paper with an HB pencil.

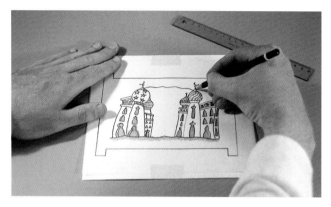

2 Remove the tracing paper from the photocopied image. Turn the tracing paper so that the pencil lines of the image are underneath. Taking a soft pencil, e.g. a B pencil, rub over the image area, covering it completely with graphite.

3 Turning the tracing paper so that the pencil outline of the image is uppermost, attach it to the paper which you wish to transfer the image onto. Carefully draw over the image again. You will create a light impression of the image on your paper which you can decorate or paint as you wish. You can remove any unnecessary marks with an eraser. **a**

b

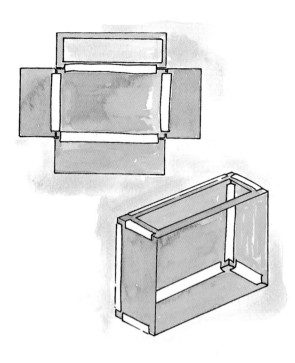

MAKING AND COVERING BOXES

Some of the projects feature designs using boxes as a part of their basic structure, e.g. the Three-Dimensional Theatre Picture and the Opera House. I use a very simple technique for making boxes, which is ideal if the box is going to be covered, using strips of paper, coated with glue, to join the pieces together. Bookbinders' webbing, which is readily available from art and craft shops, can also be used. It is more durable and stronger than ordinary.

1 Lay all the pieces needed for the box flat in the order they need to be attached together. Cut strips of paper, about 1in (25mm) wide, and coat them with glue. Use these strips to join the four main seams.

2 Fold to form a box shape and continue to join the seams, using strips of glued paper both inside and out. Leave the box to dry completely before covering.

PRESENTATION BOXES

All of the presentation boxes, apart from the portfolio-style box suggested for the Folding Theatre in a Box, are constructed using a very simple technique. The style of the presentation box I've suggested is unusual because it does not have a base. The box slides over the top of the theatre, and the base of the theatre itself becomes the bottom of the box. The box is not fixed to the theatre base, so will lift off easily. Unlike the portfolio case, this type of box acts more as a cover than a carrying case.

In some of the designs featured in this book, the base of the theatre is made out of a box, e.g. the Theatre in a Matchbox. The theatre framework and scenery can be stored neatly away in the box when not in use. If the box used is not a standard size, e.g. matchbox size, templates have been provided to help you make up the basic boxes.

1 Use the dimensions given on the project templates to cut the following pieces: two side pieces, one top piece and front and back pieces.

2 Cover one side of each of the box pieces with a decorative image of your choice. I have provided a decorative sheet, of music (see page 105), which can be enlarged and photocopied onto coloured paper. Colourwashing or tea staining can also give an attractive effect.

3 Cut four 1in (25mm) strips of the same decorated paper you used to cover the box pieces. Lay the box pieces out in the following order with the decorated side facing downwards: side, front, side, back. Make sure that the sections are laid close together, so there are no gaps between them.

4 Apply glue to the decorated side of three of the strips. Lay the strips so that they join each piece together as shown. When the glue is completely dry, trim off the excess paper at the top and bottom of the strips.

5 Bring the two remaining edges of the box together. Apply a layer of glue to the decorated side of the last strip and lay it underneath the two remaining edges of the box. Press the edges of the box firmly together to ensure no gap is left. Leave the glue to dry, then trim off the excess strip.

6 Take the top section of the box and draw two diagonal lines from corner to corner. This will enable you to locate the centre of the top piece. Make a small hole where the lines join and attach a decorative knob or handle.

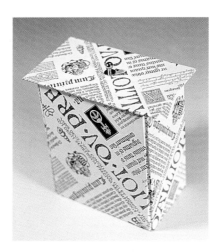

7 Apply glue along the edges of the undecorated side of the top piece and carefully attach it to the main body of the box. The box can then be slotted easily over the theatre, so its bottom edge rests on the theatre base.

MAKING SIMPLE CURTAIN GUIDES

The simplest form of curtain guide consists of two rectangles of card, placed either side of the back of the proscenium opening. One rectangle is slightly smaller than the other. The two shapes are glued together so that their long edges are flush on one side. The smaller rectangle is sandwiched between the back of the proscenium arch and the larger rectangle of card, creating a small groove which the curtain can slide into.

CREATING THREE-DIMENSIONAL EFFECTS

The technique used in the theatre projects to create visual depth can be compared to the popular technique of three-dimensional decoupage. A number of copies are made of one image, and certain parts of each copy of the image are cut out. The copies are then arranged in layers so that the viewer can see through one layer to the next. In three-dimensional decoupage special silicone glue is used to hold the layers slightly apart.

In the toy theatre, the same principle is used to create depth. Layers of scenery with parts cut away are arranged from the front to the back of the stage, leaving some space in between each layer. The result is an exciting three-dimensional effect, creating a feeling of depth for the viewer.

In the cases of projects like the Theatre in a Matchbox and the Pop-up Theatre Greetings Card, the effect is achieved by using the different scenery images. The front scene has a large opening cutting away, while the last sheet of scenery, just before the backdrop, has a small opening.

The decoupage technique becomes a little more complicated when only one scenery image is used, as is the case with the Folding Theatre in a Box and the Three-dimensional Theatre Picture. When only using one scenery image, it is best to choose an image that has been drawn in perspective. Having decided on the number of layers you want to have (I have suggested an exact number for each of the theatre projects), you will need to decide which parts will be removed from each layer. You will find the scenery sheet nearest to the front needs to have more material removed, whilst the last layer, which will form the backdrop, can be left complete.

If you are unsure which part of the scenery image to cut away in each layer, try shading the area with pencil or a black marker, this way you will ensure that you do not cut too much away. Start with the back scenery sheet and work forwards, cutting away a little more of the image with each layer you get to.

MAKING SIMPLE MOVEMENTS

I've introduced some simple moving pieces to two of the theatre projects to add interest to the finished design.

Punch and Judy Booth (see page 75). This design features a simple rocking device. The pivots, on which the moving pieces rock to and fro, are made with split pins, which are readily available from your local stationery shop. To ensure that the rocking movement is smooth, make sure that the pins are not fixed in too tight.

Opera House (see page 51). The theatre stage of this design has grooves which allow characters to move back and forth across the stage. Four guiding channels are created inside the stage before the surface of the stage is put in place. Squares of card, attached to bamboo skewers, are placed inside the channels so that they can slide back and forth. Once the top of the stage is in place the characters can be attached to the squares of card. The ends of the bamboo skewers are decorated with wooden balls.

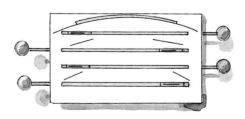

DECORATIVE TECHNIQUES

Colourwashing

Colourwashing is a simple technique. Inks or paints are watered down and applied with a brush or sponge to large surfaces of paper (or photocopied images). Beautiful effects and shades of colour can be achieved by experimenting with the ratio of water to colouring medium. Do not panic if the paper wrinkles, it will flatten out as it dries.

Colourwashing a photocopied image with blue ink

Metallic effects

Metallic paints, foil-backed papers and transfer metal leafing can produce a luxurious finish, giving your theatre a touch of glamour.

Transfer metal leafing is a gilding technique. Metal leafing is surprisingly inexpensive when you consider the beautiful finishes it can achieve. The cheapest, and yet most convincing, metallic leafing is Dutch metal leaf. Metal leafing is available in most craft outlets in a variety of different metals – gold, aluminium, copper and pewter. They usually come in books of about 25 sheets, which will go a long way. Using metallic foiling is quite simple, but remember that the leafing is delicate and needs careful handling.

1 Coat the image, paper or part of the theatre that is to be gilded with a thin covering of varnish, diluted glue or, preferably, acrylic gold size, a special glue for attaching metallic foiling. Some types of metallic foiling come in a pack with their own adhesive.

2 Apply the foiling to the varnish or glue, immediately smoothing out any bubbles. Peel the waxed backing paper off the foiling and burnish with a soft brush or cloth. If using acrylic gold size as an adhesive, wait fifteen minutes for the wet, white glue surface to go clear and tacky, then apply the transfer metal leaf as before.

The advantage of acrylic gold size is that it stays tacky for 24 hours, allowing you more working time for bigger projects. You can fill in any missed patches with metal leaf scraps and then varnish your gilding for posterity.

Rubber stamping

Homemade rubber stamps are an economical way to repeat a decorative image. A simple, but effective way of making rubber stamps is to use rubber sheeting, which is freely available in craft outlets, and an appropriate material for the base, such as a block of card, a cork sanding block or an empty plastic film roll container (ideal for small images).

Draw the required image on thin rubber sheeting. Cut around the image with a scalpel or small scissors and glue to your chosen base.

When printing with your stamp, apply paint with a small roller or use a commercial ink pad. Ink pads are available in a vast array of exquisite colours from art and craft shops.

I used the rubber stamping technique to create the gold scroll image on the front of the stage in Theatre Grande project. Instead of using ink or paint to colour the image, I applied acrylic gold size with a rubber stamp. When the acrylic gold size was tacky, I applied Dutch gold leaf, then burnished it with a soft cloth (a soft brush could also be used).

Using rubber stamping and transfer metal leafing

A scraperboard proscenium arch design.

Scraperboard (scratchboard)

Scraperboard or scratchboard is thought of by many as an old-fashioned technique, this could not be further from the truth. Scraperboard has made a welcome comeback and is the favourite medium of many illustrators around the world.

Scraperboard is available from art and craft shops (see page 20 for more details about the types of scraperboard available). The best results are achieved by using a set of scraperboard tools, which are specially made to produce different effects on the board. The finished result is a striking and dramatic black and white image, which reproduces well when photocopied.

The black scraperboard technique was used to create the decorative templates for the Folding Theatre in a Box and the Opera House. Try designing your own proscenium arch using this technique.

Tea staining

Leave six or more tea bags to stew in a bowl of boiling water and you will create a strong natural dye that is hard to recreate using paints and inks. Tea dye dries beautifully patchy, turning ordinary photocopies into antique manuscripts within seconds. Apply two or more coats of tea, leaving pools of dye to dry darker. Splashing and streaking the dye adds to the effect.

A similar effect can be achieved by using a strong solution of instant coffee. Or you can try sprinkling a few granules of coffee onto an image which has been washed with a light surface of water to create an interesting effect. Do not forget, the more dye you apply the deeper the colour will be.

Tea staining adds an antique look

PART II

PROJECTS

CHAPTER SEVEN

THEATRE IN A MATCHBOX

This is a charming, yet surprisingly simple project. All the components of this miniature theatre pack neatly away into the matchbox, which also forms the basis of the theatre structure. The outer sleeve of the box is covered in a stylish music motif. The inner sleeve, which acts as the stage, is decorated with ornamental scrolls and an orchestra pit.

The theatre framework consists of a proscenium arch which has a decorative pediment, a back wall and scenery supports. The magic castle set, made up of a backdrop and three scenery sheets, is delicately painted with inks and watercolours. The framework is simply fixed to the stage using tabs and the scenery is hung from the supports. The result is an exquisite theatre in miniature – a beautiful gift for anyone.

Techniques

Materials

Household-size matchbox, 4¾in x 2⅝in x 1in
(120mm x 66mm x 25mm), or an A3 sheet of white card,
190/200gsm, to make your own box
White card or Bristol board, 300gsm, A3 sheet
Blue paper, suitable for photocopying
Red paper, suitable for photocopying
Watercolour inks, paints or a colouring medium of your choice

Decorative photocopies, enlarge by 200%
One copy of proscenium arch and pediment on blue paper 104–5
Two copies of stage on blue paper
One copy of music on blue paper
One copy of curtain on red paper
One copy of music on red paper
One copy each of four scenery sheets on white paper

Theatre structure checklist

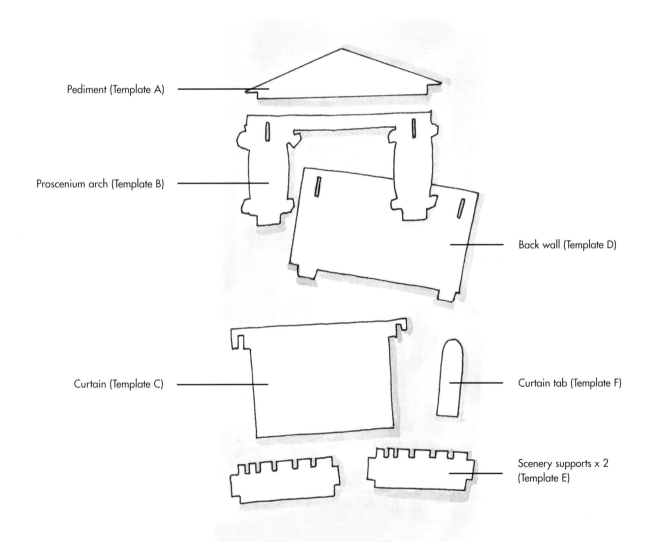

Pediment (Template A)

Proscenium arch (Template B)

Back wall (Template D)

Curtain (Template C)

Curtain tab (Template F)

Scenery supports x 2
(Template E)

Theatre Structure

Turn to the templates on page 106. Photocopy the templates, enlarging them by 200%, then use your photocopied templates to cut the theatre structure of white card or Bristol board. Make sure that you also lightly trace the markings and notes on to the pieces in pencil.

If you don't have a matchbox the right size, photocopy Templates G and H and cut these shapes out of 190/200gsm white card.

1 To make the matchbox, take the inner box (Template G) and score it along the lines indicated. Fold the sides of the box up, folding the side tabs in. Glue the tabs to the ends of the box. Fold down the end flaps and glue them down over the tabs. Score and fold the box sleeve (Template H) and apply glue carefully where indicated by the template.

2 Cover the box sleeve of your matchbox with the blue music photocopy. Make sure the join of the paper is at the side of the box.

3 Decorate the sides of the box sleeve, one side with the orchestra, one with scroll and leaves both cut from the spare blue photocopy of the stage.

4 Cut and fold the stage image as indicated and use it to cover the inner box.

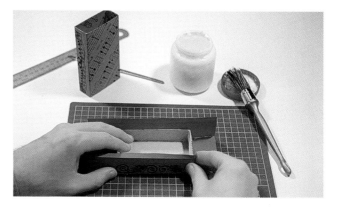

5 You will need to make four narrow slits at the four corners of the stage to accommodate the tabs on the proscenium arch and back wall. See Template G for the exact position of these slits.

6 Using PVA or spray mount, glue the decorative photocopies of the proscenium arch and pediment to the correct white card pieces and trim them carefully with a scalpel and metal rule. Cover the back wall with the red photocopied music image. Cover the scenery supports with the blue photocopied music image.

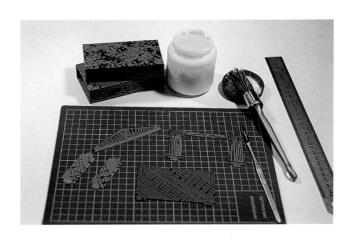

7 Cut narrow slits in the proscenium arch and the back wall as indicated by the template. These slits will accommodate the tabs on the scenery supports.

8 Cover the curtain (Template C) and curtain tab (Template F) with spare pieces of red or blue photocopied paper. The curved curtain tab allows the curtain to be dropped in, and lifted out of place easily. After the tab has been covered, score it and bend it into a curve as shown (see below). Staple the curtain tab on to the back of the curtain. You can then decorate the curtain with a silver pen.

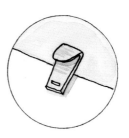

9 Construct the theatre by attaching the proscenium arch and back wall to the stage using their tabs. The scenery supports can then be attached between the back wall and proscenium arch, using the slits made in Step 7. The pediment should be placed behind the proscenium arch and in front of the scenery supports to keep it in position.

10 Glue the scenery photocopies onto white card, trimming them with a scalpel and metal rule. Carefully cut away the excess card inside each of the scenery pieces using a scalpel.

11 The scenery is now ready for colouring. I used watercolour paints but the choice is yours, use whatever you feel comfortable with.

12 Drop the scenery and backdrop into place. Finally, drop in the curtain and your Theatre in a Matchbox is finished.

When the theatre comes apart, the different pieces should fit snugly into the stage, which in turn slips easily into the outer sleeve of the matchbox, making a perfect present for your family or friends.

Future projects to try yourself
When you have completed this project, why not design a theatre in a matchbox yourself? Give yourself a real challenge and try to fit a beautiful theatre in to the smallest box that you can find. It can be done – I have seen some stunning designs and your latest creation will make a great conversation piece.

CHAPTER EIGHT

FOLDING THEATRE IN A BOX

THIS toy theatre was inspired by the peephole and folding theatres of the nineteenth century. When the theatre is extended, the magic garden scene is given depth and the illusion of perspective. It can also fold flat easily and fit into its stylish portfolio-style presentation box. A unique present, the Folding Theatre in a Box can be sent safely through the post when a special occasion demands.

Techniques

Materials

Black micro-corrugated card, ¹⁄₁₆in thick (1.5mm), 3 sheets of A2
Black card, 200gsm, A3 sheet
White card, 200gsm, A3 sheet
Dark blue paper, 80gsm, A4 sheet

Decorative photocopies, enlarge by 200%

Three copies of scenery image (Template B) on white paper

Theatre structure

Turn to the templates on page 108. Draw the templates using the dimensions given. Make sure that you also transfer any markings.

Theatre structure checklist

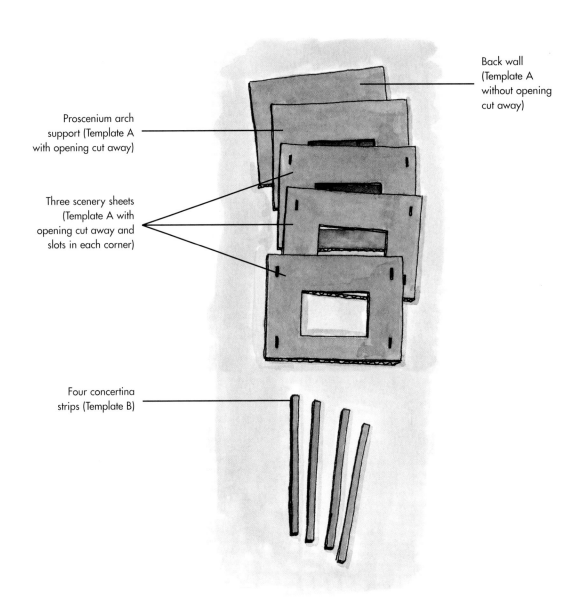

Back wall (Template A without opening cut away)

Proscenium arch support (Template A with opening cut away)

Three scenery sheets (Template A with opening cut away and slots in each corner)

Four concertina strips (Template B)

1 Mount the proscenium arch photocopy onto one of the black micro-corrugated card pieces and cut the away the proscenium opening.

2 Take three black micro-corrugated card pieces and cut four slits in each, one in each corner, as marked on Template A. It is important that the slits are in exactly the same place on every card. The concertina strips will be threaded through the slits, pulling the theatre together. Once the slits are cut, remove the opening of each of the three card pieces.

3 Cover the remaining piece of micro-corrugated card with blue paper on one side, creating a midnight sky backdrop. I added a burst of stars to my backdrop using a simple stencil and some silver spray paint.

a

b

4 Mount the three scenery images onto white card. Trim each scene down, ensuring that you leave a border to glue the scene to its supporting micro-corrugated card piece. Cut different areas out of each scene to create a three-dimensional effect when the scenes are put together (for more detailed advice see page 26).

5 The scenery images can then be attached to their supporting black micro-corrugated card pieces, fitting over the opening which was cut away in Step 2.

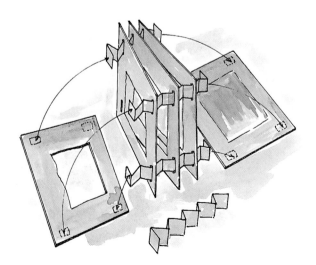

6 Score the concertina strips every ¾in (19mm), as marked in Template B, with a scoring tool or empty biro. Fold to form the concertina supports.

7 Thread the concertina strips through the slits in the scenery support cards. Make sure that you thread the cards in the right order. Glue the ends of the strips to the backdrop and proscenium arch.

The finished theatre is an ideal gift for family and friends. You can enhance your gift further by making a portfolio-style box

MAKING A PORTFOLIO-STYLE BOX

Extra equipment
Circle cutter
Rivets and a rivet tool

Materials
Black micro-corrugated card, 1/16in (1.5mm) thick
Black raffia string

Decorative photocopy
One copy of the proscenium arch (on page 107) reduced by 50%

Box structure
The basic structure of the box is formed out of one piece, Template E on page 109. Make a copy using the dimensions given on a large piece of scrap paper. Use this template to mark up and cut the piece out of micro-corrugated card.

Templates C and D make up the fastening of the box. Draw these using the dimensions given.

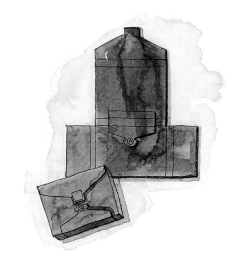

1 Score along the lines marked on the three pieces you have cut out using a scoring tool or empty biro.

2 Using a rivet tool, attach the circle (Template C) to the other fastening piece (Template D) using the illustration as a guide (see right). Different brands of rivet tool operate slightly differently, so you will need to read the manufacturer's instructions carefully before you use it.

3 Glue the two riveted pieces to the basic structure of the box (Template E) using the diagram as a guide (see right).

4 Cut out the proscenium arch image and a piece of black micro-corrugated card so that they are the same size. Glue the two pieces together, fixing a short length of black raffia in between the photocopied image and the card. To fasten the box, twist the raffia around the card circle.

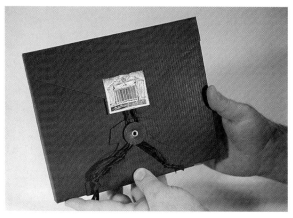

Future projects to try yourself
After being inspired by this project, why not try making an alternative folding theatre in a box, where the base and the box lid are actually part of the theatre? The box lid can be removed entirely revealing the proscenium arch, or it can even double as a proscenium arch. Try fitting some kind of curtain so the set cannot be seen when the box is closed.

CHAPTER NINE

POP-UP THEATRE GREETINGS CARD

This project offers a fascinating and economical way to make a card for a special occasion.

Using the colourful theme of arabesque, invoking exotic images of Arabian nights, this simple pop-up card is transformed with some delicate watercolour artwork creating a colourful scene of a desert town. One of the advantages of this theatre design is that it can be sent through the post.

Techniques

Materials

Cold-pressed watercolour paper, 300gsm (140lbs), 2 sheets of A2
Watercolour paints or inks or colouring medium of your choice
White card or Bristol board, 300gsm, A2 sheet

Decorative photocopies, enlarge by 200%
One copy of proscenium arch 110–111
One copy each of scenery images 1, 2, 3
One copy of backdrop
One copy each of curtain images 1 and 2

Theatre structure

Turn to the templates on page 112. Draw the templates using the dimensions given. Use your templates to cut the pieces out of white card or Bristol board.

Theatre structure checklist

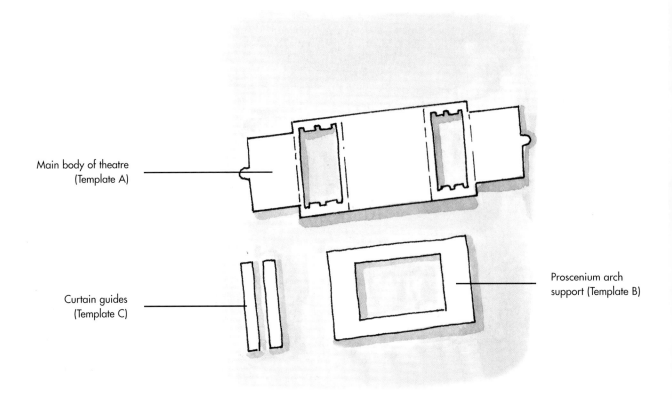

Main body of theatre
(Template A)

Curtain guides
(Template C)

Proscenium arch
support (Template B)

1 Transfer the three scenery images, two curtain images and backdrop on watercolour paper using the tracing method demonstrated on page 23. Once the images have been transferred colour the backdrop and curtains section using a colouring medium of your choice, and leave to dry flat. I used watercolour paints. Back all these pieces, except for the backdrop, with 300gsm white card.

2 Score and fold the main body of the theatre (Template A) along lines indicated. This will create the back section and scenery supports. Glue the backdrop to the back of the theatre. Then glue the curtains to the curtain supports as shown.

3 Colour the scenery images with a colouring medium of your choice. Allow them to dry completely, then cut away the part of each scene to create a three-dimensional effect (for more detailed advice see page 26).

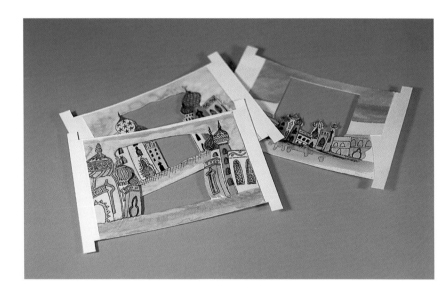

4 Slide each scene in turn into the scenery support slots, until all scenery is in place. Scenery image 1 goes at the front, and scenery image 3 goes at the back.

a

b

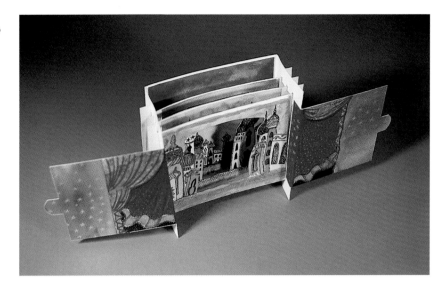

5 Attach the two curtain guides to the back of the proscenium arch support so that they are flush with the proscenium opening. Don't glue them down completely, just put a dab of glue at the top and bottom of the guides, so that the curtain can slip underneath them.

6 Transfer the proscenium arch on to watercolour paper using the tracing method as before. Colour the proscenium arch image with a colouring medium of your choice. Again, I used watercolour paints. Once the proscenium arch is completely dry, cut away the opening. Don't cut away the pieces between the pillars.

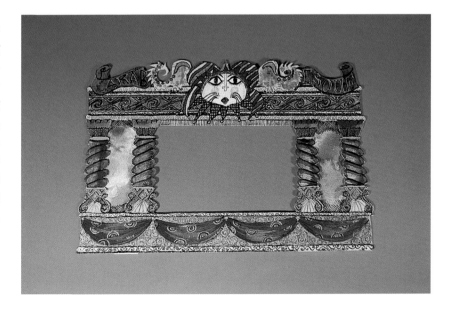

7 Mount the proscenium arch image on the proscenium arch support and slide the curtains under the curtain guides.

8 When you close the curtains, the theatre will lie flat enough to fit in to an envelope.

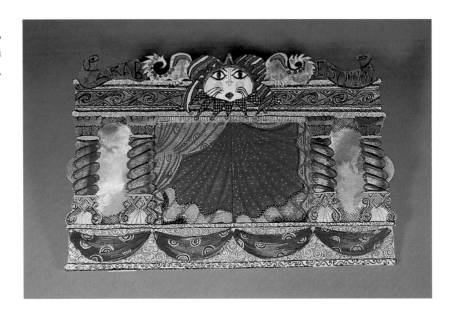

9 When the tabs are pulled the curtains will open causing the theatre to pop up into a three-dimensional object.

Future projects to try yourself
Now you are familiar with a basic pop-up construction, you can adapt this design to suit any occasion.

CHAPTER TEN

OPERA HOUSE

Housed in an attractive monochrome box, this fantasy opera house, inspired by Spanish folklore, has a simple system allowing the dancers to move across the stage. The rustic village setting against a brilliant blue sky adds a dramatic and atmospheric touch.

Techniques	
Photocopying	22
Making and covering boxes	24
Making simple curtain guides	26
Making simple movements	27

Materials

Corrugated card, $\frac{3}{32}$in (2mm) thick, 6 sheets of A3
(The three sheets should be glued together to make one sheet of three-ply card, the others can be left as single sheets)
Black corrugated card, $\frac{1}{16}$in (1.5mm) thick, A2 sheet
Box card, 800gsm, A2 sheet
Sky blue card, 240gsm, A4 sheet
Silver spray paint
Four bamboo skewers, $\frac{3}{32}$in (2mm) thick
Four wooden beads, $\frac{3}{8}$in (9.5mm) thick

Decorative photocopies, enlarge by 200% on white paper
One copy of the proscenium arch 113
One copy of curtain
One copy of curtain wings
One copy of the backdrop
One copy of scenery wings
One copy of characters (actual size)
Photocopies for covering
Five copies of the proscenium arch, enlarged to A3
Five copies of curtain image, enlarged to A3

Theatre structure

Turn to the templates on pages 114–116. Draw the templates using the dimensions given. Use your templates to cut the theatre structure out of three-ply corrugated card.

Theatre structure checklist

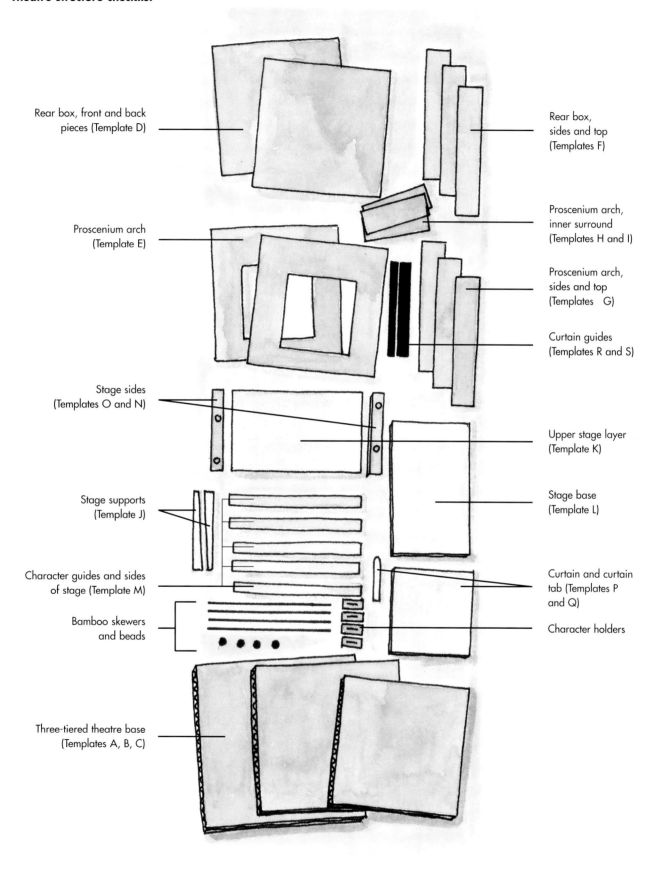

Rear box, front and back pieces (Template D)

Rear box, sides and top (Templates F)

Proscenium arch (Template E)

Proscenium arch, inner surround (Templates H and I)

Proscenium arch, sides and top (Templates G)

Curtain guides (Templates R and S)

Stage sides (Templates O and N)

Upper stage layer (Template K)

Stage supports (Template J)

Stage base (Template L)

Character guides and sides of stage (Template M)

Curtain and curtain tab (Templates P and Q)

Bamboo skewers and beads

Character holders

Three-tiered theatre base (Templates A, B, C)

1 Make the base for the theatre by cutting the top, middle and lower theatre bases (Templates A, B and C) out of three-ply corrugated card. Cover each piece in enlarged decorative photocopies. Glue them together to create a three-tiered base.

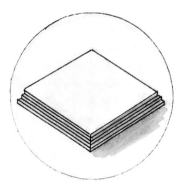

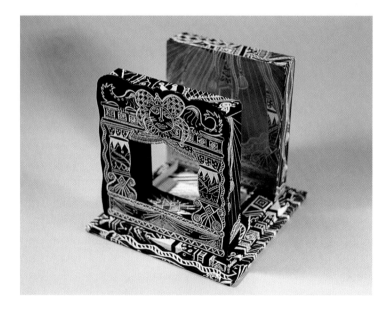

2 The main structure of the theatre is constructed from two simple boxes made from corrugated card. Cut the front, sides and back pieces out of single-ply corrugated card. Use the method described on page 24 to join the pieces together. Hold the boxes in shape with masking tape until the glue has dried. The rear box, which has no opening becomes the back wall. The front box has an opening, and forms the support for the proscenium arch. After constructing the boxes, cover them completely with the enlarged photocopy. I added a starburst of photocopied image to the inside bottom of the proscenium arch. When the boxes are finished, glue them firmly to the theatre base.

3 Mount the proscenium arch photocopy on black micro-corrugated card and glue it to the front box. Mount the curtain wing photocopies on black micro-corrugated card and attach them at an angle on the inside of the proscenium opening.

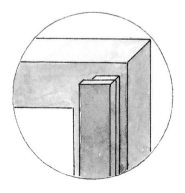

4 Cut the curtain guides (Template R and S) from 1400gsm box card and attach them either side of proscenium opening, on the reverse of the front box (see page 26 for detailed guidance).

5 Cut the stage supports from 1400gsm box card, and secure them between the front and back sections of the theatre as shown. I cut a couple of layers of corrugated card into small rectangles and glued them against the support and the theatre base, to hold the pieces in place.

6 Cut the stage pieces (Templates K, L, M, N and O) out of box card. Cover the sides in photocopy, making sure you punch the holes marked on the template.

7 Glue the sides (Template N and O) and character guides (Template M) to the stage base (Template L). As in Step 2, use strips of paper painted with glue to hold the pieces together. Ensure that the strips are inside the box, so that they do not show.

8 Cut the bamboo skewers down to 4¾in (120mm) and paint them black. Pass the skewers through the holes made in the sides of the stage. Paint the four wooden beads black and glue them to the ends of the skewers. Attach each skewer to a small block of card with strong adhesive. Check that the blocks of card run smoothly within the character guides on the base of the stage.

9 Mount the characters onto some scrap card (about 190gsm) and fix each character to a block of card by making a small incision with a scalpel, and gluing the tab of the character into the small slit for support.

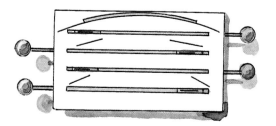

10 Cover the upper stage floor with enlarged photocopy and spray it with silver paint until the theatre image just shows through. Cut out the slits, as shown on the template. Carefully place the upper stage floor over the characters making sure there is one character in each track, and attach to the stage base. The stage is now complete and the characters should slide freely in their grooves.

11 To make the set, glue a narrow strip of 1400gsm box card to the back of the stage in a slight curve as shown. Trim the A4 sheet of sky blue card to a manageable backdrop size. Glue the backdrop scene to the sky blue card and glue this to the curved support already in place. Mount the four scenery wings onto white card and, using small tabs of card, glue them into position.

12 The finished stage is ready to glue into place. Glue along the edges of the stage supports and slide the stage into place.

13 Mount the curtain image on to 800gsm box card, attach a lifting tab and slide into place using the curtain guides.

MAKING THE PRESENTATION BOX

Materials
Box card, 1400gsm, A2 sheet
Silver handle

Box structure checklist
Box top (Template T)
Box sides (Template U)

To make up the box, follow the instructions given on page 24.
Use the box label given in the decorative photocopy section to
finish the box.

Future projects for you to try
The proscenium arch for this project was designed using
scraperboard. Why not try the scraperboard technique for
yourself and design your own proscenium arch? Try
photocopying your finished image onto coloured or textured
paper – this can create some spectacular effects.

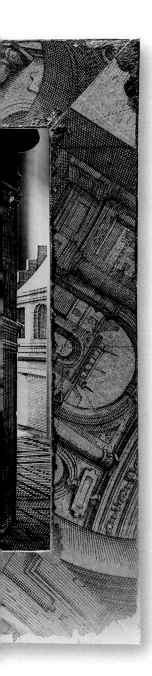

CHAPTER ELEVEN

THREE-DIMENSIONAL THEATRE PICTURE

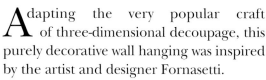

Adapting the very popular craft of three-dimensional decoupage, this purely decorative wall hanging was inspired by the artist and designer Fornasetti.

This is a superb gift idea for the person who has everything. The framed three-dimensional theatre has a strikingly effective perspective and depth. A medieval crown and frame are finished with aluminium transfer leaf, giving the theatre a regal touch.

Techniques

Materials

Corrugated card, ⅛in (3mm) thick, 3 sheets of A2
White card, 200gsm, A2 sheet
Light blue card, 100gsm, A4 sheet
Aluminium transfer leaf
Acrylic gold size
Silver spray paint
Black ink
Picture hanger

Decorative photocopies, enlarge by 200%

Theatre structure

Turn to the templates on page 118. Draw the templates using the dimensions given. Use your templates to cut the structure out of the relevant material.

Theatre structure checklist

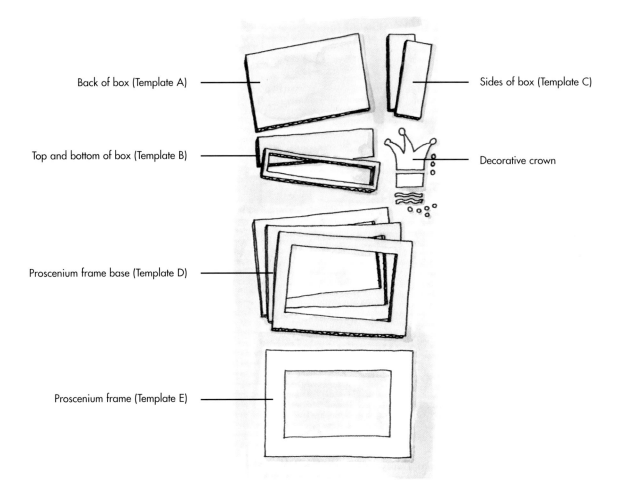

Back of box (Template A)

Sides of box (Template C)

Top and bottom of box (Template B)

Decorative crown

Proscenium frame base (Template D)

Proscenium frame (Template E)

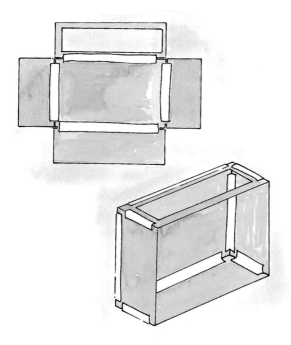

1 Cut the sides, top and back of the box (Templates A, B and C) out of corrugated card. Cut the middle section out of the top of the box (as marked on Template B). Assemble the box using strips of paper painted with glue and allow to dry (for more detailed advice see page 24).

2 Cut wide strips of photocopied image and use it to cover the box, gluing the paper on carefully.

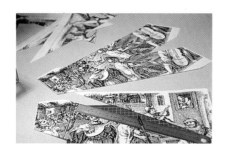

a

b

3 Mount the five photocopies of the scenery image onto white card and carefully cut them out. Each image has a different amount cut away (see page 26).

4 Cut card struts from corrugated card. Each strip is about 4¾in x ⅝in strips (120mm x 16mm). Fix the card struts to the back of each scenery sheet, to hold the sheets apart, and add to the three-dimensional effect. Glue the backdrop to the sky blue sheet of paper. I gave the tiled floor a more pronounced chequered effect by going over the design with black ink.

5 Working from the back forwards, place each mounted scenery image into the box in sequence. Put the front scenery image in place.

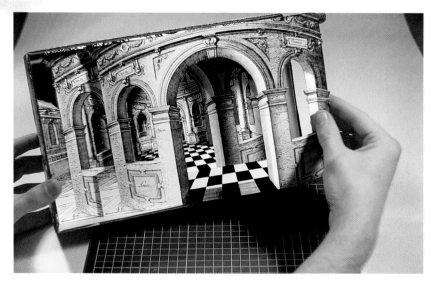

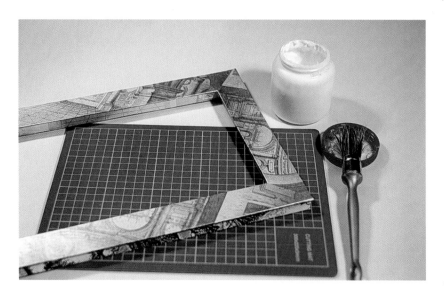

6 Glue the three copies of Template D firmly together to make a three-ply corrugated card proscenium frame base. When the proscenium frame base is dry cover it, and the proscenium frame, with the enlarged scenery image. Glue the frame to the base. When the glue is dry, spray the frame and base with a light coat of silver spray paint, so that the black and white scenery image just shows through.

7 Fix the whole frame securely to the front of the box. Fix the picture hanger to the back of the theatre using a strong adhesive, such as two-part epoxy glue.

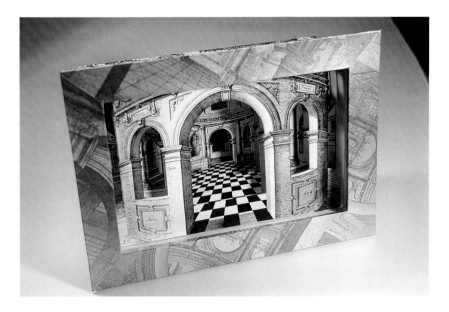

8 Photocopy the decorative crown, enlarging it by 273%. Cut the crown shape, base and decorations out of thin white card. Fold the rectangle shape along the dotted lines. Glue the tabs created to the crown shape to create a curved base. Glue the wavy lines to the curved base and the small circles to the top of the crown. Paint these pieces with acrylic gold size and cover them with aluminium transfer leaf. Fix the crown to the centre of the top of the frame.

9 The outside and inside edges of the frame can also be decorated with aluminium transfer leaf, creating an antique and distressed look which is extremely desirable and attractive.

Future projects for you to try
You can use the techniques found in this project to design and make numerous three-dimensional pictures. Once you have found the image that you like, the rest is simple.

CHAPTER TWELVE

WINTER WONDERLAND

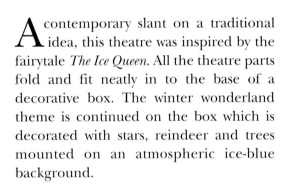

A contemporary slant on a traditional idea, this theatre was inspired by the fairytale *The Ice Queen*. All the theatre parts fold and fit neatly in to the base of a decorative box. The winter wonderland theme is continued on the box which is decorated with stars, reindeer and trees mounted on an atmospheric ice-blue background.

Techniques

Materials

Box card, 1400gsm, 2 sheets of A2
Blue card, 240gsm, A2 sheet
Red card, 240gsm, A2 sheet
Black card, 240gsm, A2 sheet
White card, 300gsm, A2 sheet
Paper-backed silver foil, 4 sheets of A4
Red corrugated card, A4 sheet
Black decorative paper, A2 sheet
Deep blue tissue paper, A2 sheet
Silver grey craft paper
Black silk tissue paper
Light blue foil, A4 sheet
Dark blue foil, A4 sheet
Silver and black inks
Silver, blue and purple colouring pencils

Decorative photocopies, enlarge by 200%
Photocopy and enlarge these images on to white paper and
cut them out. Use your photocopied images as templates.
Seven copies of the stars and moons on red card,
blue foil and metallic silver paper   119–121
One copy each of the two tree images on black card
One copy of tree and reindeer image on black card
Six copies of the moose image on black card
One copy of orchestra and conductor image on
black card
Copies of audience images (one of large audience
and two of each small audience) on black card
One copy of crown image on blue card
Two copies of balcony box image on red card

Theatre structure
Turn to the templates on pages 122–125. Draw the templates
using the dimensions given. Use your templates to trace and
cut out the structure of the theatre out of 1400gsm box card.
The curtain should be cut from red corrugated card.

Theatre structure checklist

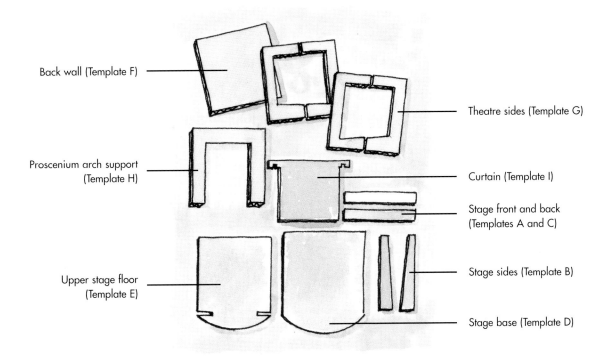

Back wall (Template F)

Theatre sides (Template G)

Proscenium arch support
(Template H)

Curtain (Template I)

Stage front and back
(Templates A and C)

Upper stage floor
(Template E)

Stage sides (Template B)

Stage base (Template D)

1 Gather together the five pieces which make up the stage
(Templates A, B, C, D and E). Cover the top of the stage base
and sides with silver grey craft paper. Cover the upper stage layer
with paper-backed silver foil. Cover the underside of the stage
base with black silk tissue paper. Glue all these covered pieces
together to form the stage. Finally, attach the large audience
image and the conductor and orchestra image, cut from the
black card, to the front edges of the stage.

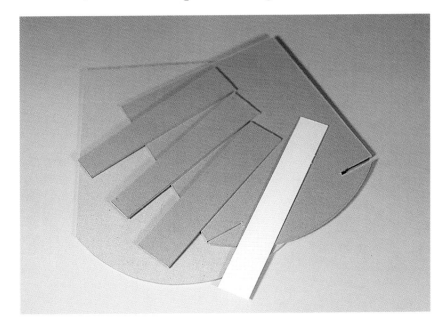

2 Cut out the pieces which form the theatre structure (Templates F, G and H). Lay out the pieces of the proscenium arch as shown. Cut 1in (25mm) wide paper strips and coat them with glue. Use these strips to join the pieces together. Join the side pieces together first. The strips of paper which form the hinges should go on the inside of the theatre structure once it is completed. Cover the outside surface of each side with black tissue paper. Fold the excess over onto the inside of the pieces. To allow the side hinges to move freely, you will need to release the excess tissue glued on the inside of the pieces by cutting a small slit.

3 Lay the back and sides flush together face down. While the pieces are lying flat, cover them with paper-backed silver foil. Cut a scalpel line through the side hinges to allow them to move freely. Any exposed board can be painted black.

4 Cover the outside of the proscenium arch support with black tissue paper, folding any excess over onto the inside of the piece. Using strips of paper, join the proscenium arch support to the sides. Cut a piece of paper-backed silver foil using Template H and glue it inside the proscenium arch support. Stand the construction up, making sure that the sides can fold inwards.

5 Cover the back wall with the pale blue foil. Decorate the backdrop with silver stars and a crescent moon cut from deep blue foil.

6 Cut the proscenium arch image from 300gsm card and cover it with blue tissue paper. Cover the back of each wing with paper-backed silver foil.

7 Cut the side flaps from blue card. Decorate the flaps with the small audience and theatre box images and add finishing touches with silver and black ink and the purple pencil. Attach the side flaps to the wings of the proscenium arch image.

8 Cut the decorative pillars from red card and cut out the slits. Back the pillars with paper-backed silver foil so that the foil shows through the slits. Decorate the pillars with silver pencil and glue them to the proscenium arch.

9 Glue the decorative proscenium arch to the proscenium arch support, making sure that the proscenium arch fits snugly into the two slots in the upper stage.

10 Cut the larger pediment piece from 300gsm card. Cover the larger piece with blue tissue paper. Cut the smaller pediment piece from red card and decorate it with silver ink, purple pencil and two stars. Attach these to the proscenium arch.

11 Cut the curtain drape from red card and decorate it with silver ink and blue and purple pencil. Glue the decorated drape to the pediment.

12 Cut the curtain layers from red card and decorate with coloured pencils. Glue the two layers together and attach them to the reverse side of the pediment to form a curtain pelmet.

13 Cut the crown from blue card and decorate with silver ink. Using a small tab of scrap card, attach the crown to the top of the pediment.

14 Attach two strips of card to the pediment as shown in the illustration (see right) so that the pediment will clip on to the top of the proscenium arch.

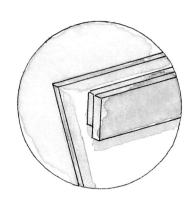

15 Mount the deer image onto black card. Make a simple stand from black card and attach the deer image to it. Cut a rectangle from corrugated card, 5in by ½in (127mm x 13mm). Cut two thin strips of corrugated card and glue them on the base strip leaving a small gap between them, just wide enough so that the reindeer scene can slip into it. Cover the stand with black ink.

16 Cut the curtain from red corrugated card and attach a silver foil tree for decoration.

17 Decorate the underside of the stage base, as it shows quite prominently when placed in the box base. I wrote 'Winter Wonderland' in silver ink and added a few stars. I also decorated the reverse side of the side flaps, covering them with silver foil and adding red and blue stars, as these show when the theatre is folded in its stand. All the components of the theatre fit into the base.

MAKING A PRESENTATION BOX

Techniques		**Materials**
Presentation boxes	24	Corrugated card, ⅛in (3mm) thick, A2 sheet

Box structure checklist

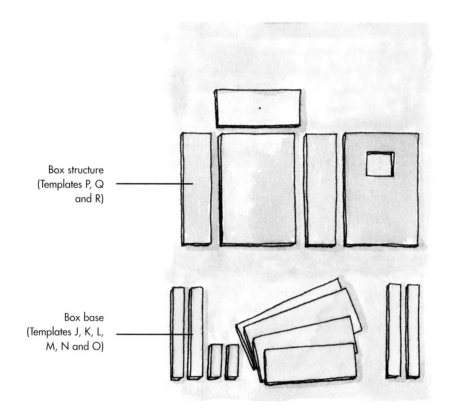

Box structure
(Templates P, Q
and R)

Box base
(Templates J, K, L,
M, N and O)

1 Cut the pieces for the box base (Templates J, K, L, M, N and O) from corrugated card. Cover the box base bottom layer (Template O) in black silk tissue paper. Cover the other pieces in silver foil. Stick the base layers on top of each other in the correct order. Construct and glue the sides of the base box, then attach the inserts inside as shown.

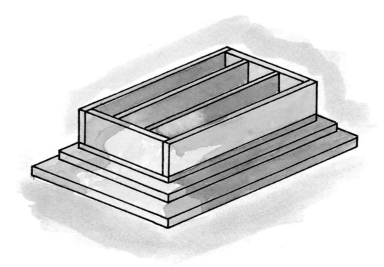

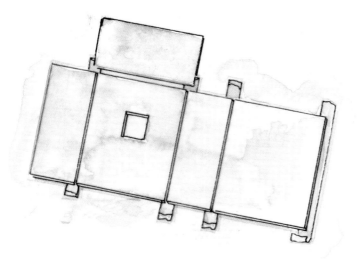

2 Construct a simple box to cover the theatre (for more detailed advice see page 24) and decorate with six moose images cut from black card. Cut a tree image from black card and attach to front over the window. Finally, add silver stars to give the box a magical touch.

Future projects for you to try
This simple construction can be used in a number of themed ideas. Why not try using a different colour scheme and decorative theme, e.g. an Autumn scene with falling leaves, or a bonfire with fireworks.

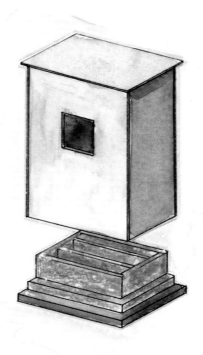

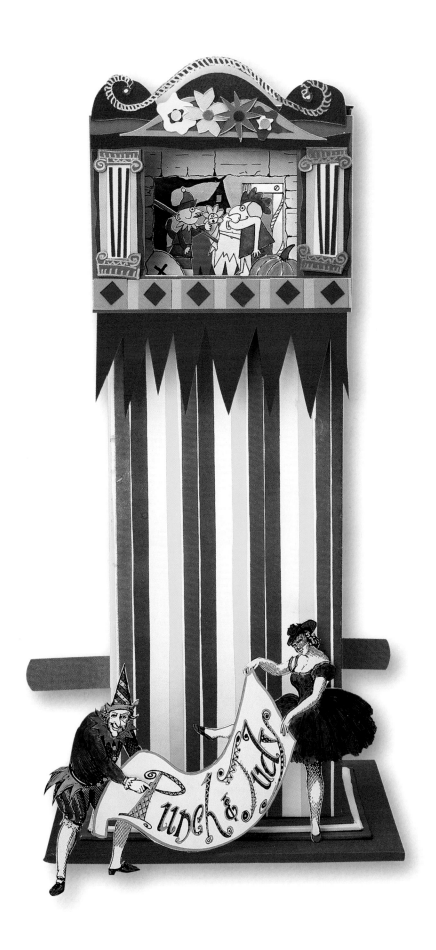

CHAPTER THIRTEEN

PUNCH AND JUDY BOOTH

No book on theatre would be complete without the lovable Punch and his long-suffering wife and baby. Inspired by childhood memories of coastal holidays, this is my view of a great British institution of puppet theatre. Sadly, very few Punch and Judy booths are to be found today.

In this theatre, a large slice of tradition is blended with a splattering of the contemporary. Punch and Judy and their entourage are displayed in highly stylized surroundings.

Techniques

Materials

Micro corrugated card, ¹⁄₁₆in (1.5 mm) thick, 2 sheets of A2
Corrugated card, ⅛in (3mm) thick, A2 sheet
White paper, 100gsm, A2 sheet, 3 sheets of A3 and 2 sheets of A4
Red card, 240gsm, A2 sheet
Dark blue card, 240gsm, A2 sheet
Pale blue card, 240gsm, A2 sheet
Yellow card, 240gsm, A2 sheet
Green card, 240gsm, A2 sheet
Pink card, 240gsm, A2 sheet
Red, blue, yellow watercolour inks
Split pins
Selection of magic markers or a colouring medium of your choice

Decorative photocopies, enlarge by 200%
All decorative photocopies onto white paper
Proscenium arch decorations cut out of coloured card
(see Step 9)   126–7
Curtain image
Four characters
Scenery images 1 and 2
Backdrop
Character decoration for theatre base

Theatre structure

Turn to the templates on pages 128–9. Using the dimensions given, measure and cut out the templates onto scrap paper (so you can use them again). Trace and mark out the score lines and other markings in pencil.

Theatre structure checklist

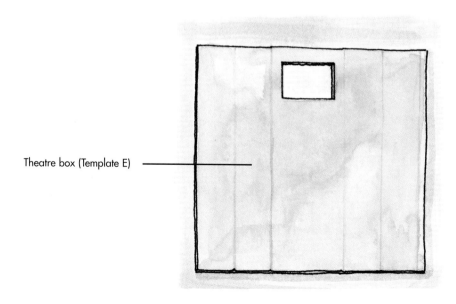

Theatre box (Template E)

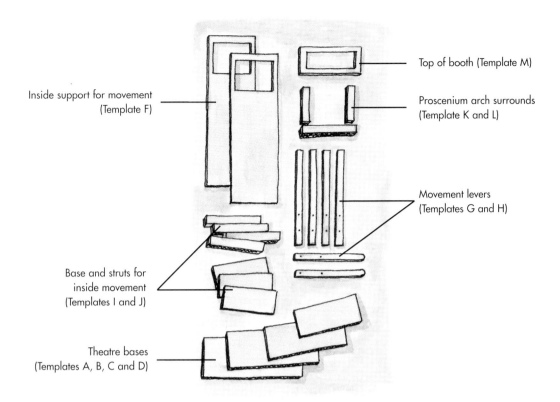

Inside support for movement
(Template F)

Top of booth (Template M)

Proscenium arch surrounds
(Template K and L)

Movement levers
(Templates G and H)

Base and struts for
inside movement
(Templates I and J)

Theatre bases
(Templates A, B, C and D)

1 Cut the four theatre bases (Templates A, B, C and D) out of corrugated card. Colourwash three sheets of A3 paper in red, blue and yellow. Cover the pieces in colourwashed paper. Cover Template A in red, Template B in yellow, Template C in blue and Template D in red. Glue the pieces together to form a tiered base.

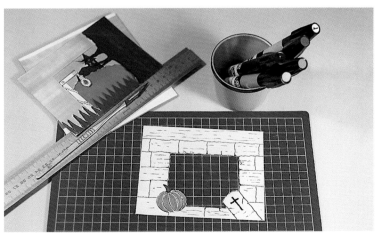

2 Mount the scenery photocopies onto white card and colour with a medium of your choice. I used coloured marker pens for this project. Cut away excess card to form the set (for detailed advice see page 26).

3 Mount the photocopy of the characters onto white card and colour them in. I used watercolour inks. Cut carefully around the characters with a scalpel. For the character decoration, which goes at the base of the theatre, I coloured the two characters, then stuck them to a banner, onto which I had traced the lettering. I decorated the lettering with inks and a gold pen.

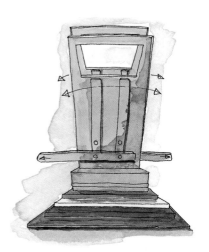

4 Construct the inside movement using the illustration as a guide.

5 Scenery image 1 should be attached to the front movement, scenery image 2 should be attached to the second sheet of the inside movement. (The backdrop is attached to the back of the booth later). Attach Punch and Judy to the levers in front of the first scenery image and the Ghost and Hangman to the second set of levers, in front of the second scenery image. Glue inside movement to the theatre base.

6 Take a sheet of A2 100gsm white paper and rule ⅜in (10mm) wide stripes lightly in pencil. Colour with watercolour inks in a sequence of red, blue, yellow and white and repeat until the paper is completely covered.

7 Cut theatre box (Template E) from micro-corrugated card. Cut away the proscenium opening and side slits and cover the piece with the hand-painted striped paper you made in Step 6. Score and fold along the lines indicated by the templates. Wrap the theatre box around the inner movement base (Template I) making sure that the tabs of the moving parts slide through the slits in the side of the booth. Glue along the back overlap to complete construction.

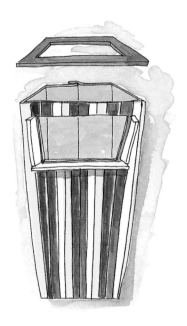

8 Glue three pieces of card around the proscenium opening as shown using paper strips. This will create a channel for the curtains.

9 Cut the proscenium arch decoration out of coloured card. Use the illustration as a guide to assembling and gluing the pieces in place.

10 Construct the curtain. Use the illustration as a guide to assembling and gluing the pieces in place.

11 Glue the backdrop to the back wall of the theatre. Glue the top into place and attach the Punch and Judy Banner to the base.

ORLANDO
FVRIOSO

CHAPTER FOURTEEN

VICTORIAN THEATRE ROYALE

This is my version of the classic toy theatres of the Victorian era. The theatre structure is covered with tea-stained paper to give it an authentic antique look. When you raise the curtains on this beautiful theatre, you discover an awe-inspiring Egyptian scene. The theatre is housed in a luxurious presentation box with brass handle.

Techniques

Materials

Corrugated card, ⅛in (3mm), 4 sheets of A2
Micro-corrugated card, 1⁄16in (1.5mm) thick, 1 sheet of A3
Corrugated card ⅛in (3mm) thick, 2 sheets of A2
Bristol board or white card, 200gsm, A2 sheet
Gold spray paint

Decorative photocopies, enlarge by 200%, except where indicated
One copy of proscenium arch — 130–1
Eight copies of proscenium arch, enlarged several
times to A3 for covering
One copy of curtain image
Two copies of curtain image, enlarged several times
to A3 for covering
One copy of perspective flooring
One copy each of the characters scenery images,
wings and backdrop

Theatre structure

Turn to the templates on pages 132–6. Draw the templates using
the dimensions given. Cut the theatre structure out of corrugated
card. Make sure that you also lightly trace the markings and
notes onto the pieces in pencil.

Theatre structure checklist

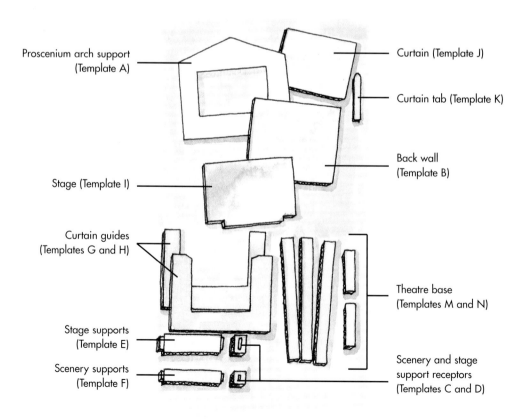

Proscenium arch support (Template A)

Curtain (Template J)

Curtain tab (Template K)

Stage (Template I)

Back wall (Template B)

Curtain guides (Templates G and H)

Theatre base (Templates M and N)

Stage supports (Template E)

Scenery supports (Template F)

Scenery and stage support receptors (Templates C and D)

1 Tea stain all the decorative photocopies, including the enlarged copies for covering the larger areas of the theatre. For more detailed instructions on tea staining, see page 30.

2 Cut the proscenium arch support (Template A) out of corrugated card. Mount the decorative proscenium arch onto Bristol board and affix it to the proscenium arch support.

3 Cut the curtain guides (Templates G and H) out of corrugated card. Glue the inner curtain guide (Template G) to reverse of the proscenium arch support, then glue the outer curtain guide (Template H) on top of the inner guide. The curtain should run in between the proscenium arch support and the outer curtain guide (for more detailed advice see page 26).

4 Cut eight of each of the stage and scenery support receptors from corrugated card. Glue four of each type of receptor together, clamp and leave to dry. Attach the receptors to the reverse side of the proscenium arch as shown. The scenery support receptors should go at the top and the stage supports should go at the bottom.

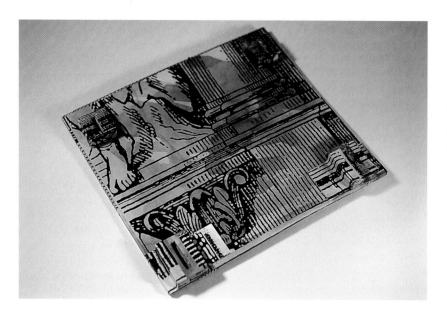

5 Cut the back wall (Template B) out of corrugated card and cover with enlarged tea-stained photocopy. Attach the stage and scenery support receptors ensuring that they correspond with the receptors on the reverse of the proscenium arch.

6 Cut four copies each of the stage and scenery supports (Templates E and F). Glue and clamp two pieces together, creating two-ply corrugated card. You should end up with four supports, two stage supports and two scenery supports. Cover them with enlarged tea-stained photocopy. Slot the stage and scenery supports in position in the back wall and proscenium arch.

a

b

7 Cut the stage (Template I) out of corrugated card and cover with enlarged tea-stained photocopy. Slide the stage into place so that it rests on the stage supports.

8 Cut the octagonal stage (Template L) out of corrugated card. Cover one side with the perspective stage image and the other side with enlarged tea-stained photocopy. Place the octagonal stage on the main stage, but do not fix it into position.

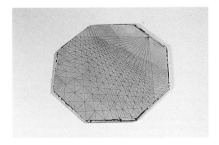

a

b

9 Mount the scenery images and wings onto Bristol board. Cut away the scenery sheets to create a three-dimensional effect (for detailed advice see page 26). Cut the four scenery support sheets (Template U) out of corrugated card and attach the scenery sheets and wings to them.

10 Hang the scenery sheets in place on the scenery supports.

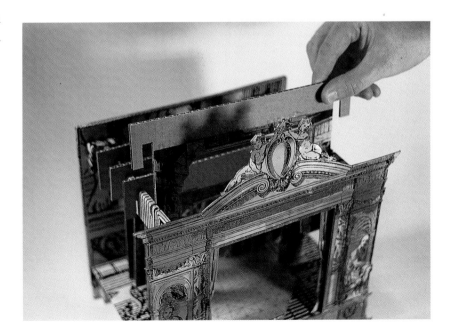

11 Cut the curtain and curtain tab (Templates J and K) out of micro-corrugated card. Cover the curtain with the decorative photocopy image and on the other side with enlarged photocopy. Cover the curtain tab with enlarged photocopy and attach to the curtain. Lower the curtain into place in between the curtain guides (see Step 3).

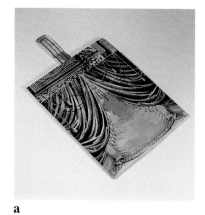

a

b

MAKING THE PRESENTATION BOX

The pieces of this theatre are designed to come apart and lie flat in a presentation box, as shown.

Materials
Corrugated card, ⅛in (3mm), 1 sheet of A2
Box card, 1400gsm, 3 sheets of A2
Gold handle

Techniques
Presentation boxes   24

Box structure checklist

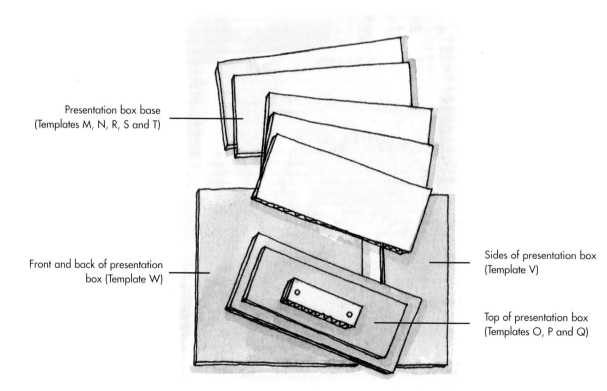

Presentation box base
(Templates M, N, R, S and T)

Front and back of presentation
box (Template W)

Sides of presentation box
(Template V)

Top of presentation box
(Templates O, P and Q)

1 Cut the pieces for the base box (Templates M, N, R, S and T) from corrugated card. Cover all the pieces in enlarged tea stained photocopy. Stick the base layers on top of each other in the correct order (Template T on the bottom, Template S in the middle and Template R on top). Glue the sides (Template M) and ends (Template N) of the base box around the top of the base (Template R).

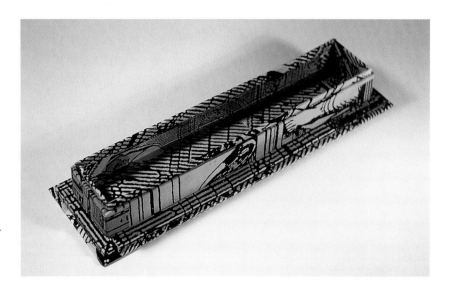

2 Cut the sides (Template V) and the front and back of the box (Template W) out of box card and cover with enlarged tea-stained photocopy. Glue the box together using the method detailed on page 24.

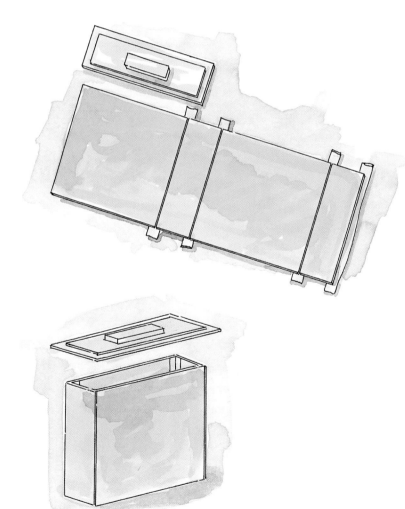

3 The lid of the box is made from three layers (Templates O, P and Q). Cut Template O from box card, cut Template P from corrugated card . Cut four copies of Template Q and glue the pieces together to form four-ply corrugated card. Cover all these pieces with enlarged tea-stained photocopy. Glue the layers together, attach the handle and, when dry, attach the lid to the rest of the box. Finish by attaching the box label (enlarged from decorative photocopies).

CHAPTER FIFTEEN

BALI SHADOW THEATRE

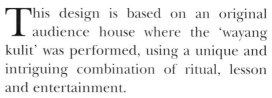

This design is based on an original audience house where the 'wayang kulit' was performed, using a unique and intriguing combination of ritual, lesson and entertainment.

In this adaptation I suggest using parchment paper or tracing paper as a substitute for the taut linen screen on which the fine filigree shadow images are projected. Traditionally shadows were created using a coconut oil lamp, but for this modern version you can use an electric light behind the screen to bring to mysterious and exotic shadows to life.

Techniques

Materials

Black micro-corrugated card, ⅟₁₆in (1.5mm) thick,
4 sheets of A2
Corrugated card, ³⁄₃₂in (2mm) thick, A2 sheet
White card, 200gsm, A2 sheet
Translucent parchment paper or tracing paper, A2 sheet
Dutch gold leaf
Acrylic gold size
Gold ink pen

Decorative photocopies

Sliding screens, enlarged by 400%
Lower edge of proscenium arch, enlarged by 400%
Shadow puppets from templates section,
enlarged by 200%

Theatre structure

Turn to the templates on page 138. Use the dimensions given to
make scrap paper templates of your own. You can then use these
templates to cut the pieces out of the relevant material.

Theatre structure checklist

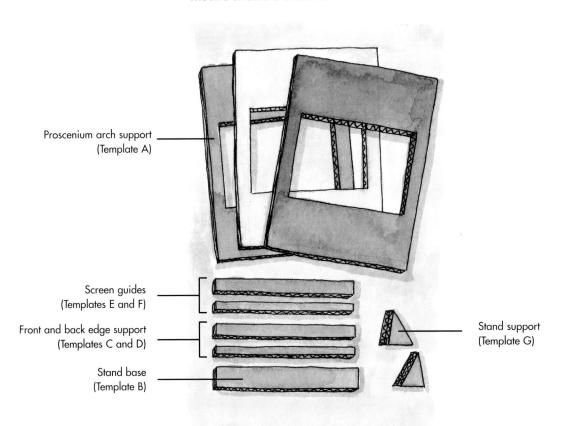

Proscenium arch support
(Template A)

Screen guides
(Templates E and F)

Front and back edge support
(Templates C and D)

Stand base
(Template B)

Stand support
(Template G)

1 Mount the enlarged photocopy of the proscenium arch image, sliding screens and lower edge of the proscenium arch onto 200gsm white card. Cut away the excess card with a scalpel.

2 Finish the edges of the decorative pieces by painting with black ink. This will give a more professional finish.

3 Cut two copies of the proscenium arch support (Template A) from black micro-corrugated card and one copy from corrugated card. Cut six copies of the inner screen guide (Template E) and four copies of the outer screen guides (Template F) from black micro-corrugated card. Glue the pieces together so that you have two three-ply inner screen guides and two two-ply outer screen guides. Attach the guides to the front of one of the black micro-corrugated proscenium arch support pieces as shown in the illustration. The guides should be positioned so that they hold the sliding screens.

4 Take the corrugated card proscenium arch support and glue a piece of translucent parchment, or thick tracing paper, across the window to create a shadow screen. Sandwich this corrugated card piece in between the two black micro-corrugated card pieces, ensuring that the screen guides are at the front. Glue the three layers together.

5 Cut three copies of the stand base from black micro-corrugated card and glue the pieces together. Cut the front edge support (Template C) and three back edge supports (Template D) out of micro-corrugated card. Glue the three back edge supports together. Cut eight copies of the stand support (Template G) and glue four pieces together to create two four-ply stand supports. The stand pieces should be glued together as shown in the diagram. The front edge support should run along the front of the stand.

6 Cut and glue translucent parchment or thick tracing paper to the front of the sliding screens.

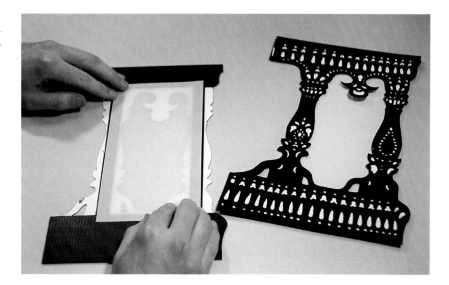

7 Slot the screens into the guide rails on the proscenium arch. The sliding screens are useful for extending the screen area, when using the theatre for shadow plays.

8 Glue the proscenium arch decoration and the lower edge of the proscenium arch to the proscenium arch support, overlapping both slightly with the sliding screens.

9 Decorate the theatre with gilding (for more details see page 28). Any pieces of black card that are exposed can be decorated with a gold pen, to match up with the surface decoration on the theatre front.

CHAPTER SIXTEEN

THEATRE GRANDE

This is the most sumptuous and decorative of my toy theatres, designed with an eccentric mix of baroque and rococo. Red drapes and cheeky cherubs rub shoulders with a unique and quirky set of characters. The traditionally plush colours of red, deep blue and royal purple are highlighted with gold leaf. The construction of this theatre looks complex, but is comparatively simple and easy to build.

Techniques

Materials

Corrugated card, ⅛in (3mm) thick, 6 sheets of A2
Grey or white card, 500gsm, 2 sheets of A2
White card, 200gsm, 2 sheets of A2
Blue tissue paper
Purple tissue paper
Red tissue paper
Orange tissue paper
Red paper, 80gsm
Acetate, A4 sheet
Watercolour inks
Prussian Blue acrylic paint
Dutch gold leaf
Acrylic gold size
Gold ink
Drawing pen
Silver and gold spray paints

Decorative photocopies, enlarge by 200%
One copy of pediment image on white paper   139–41
One copy of left and right-hand drapes and cherubs
  images on white paper
One copy of left and right-hand drapes and cherubs
  images on acetate
One copy shield image on acetate
One copy of decorative stage image on white paper
One copy of scenery image on white paper
One copy of large scroll on white paper
One of shield scroll on white paper
One copy of pelmet fringe on white paper
One copy of backdrop on white paper
One copy of characters on white paper
Fifteen copies of enlarged image (choose your own)
  on A3 white paper for covering

Theatre structure

Turn to the templates on pages 142–4. Use the dimensions given to make scrap paper templates of your own, which you can then use these templates to cut out the pieces.

Theatre structure checklist

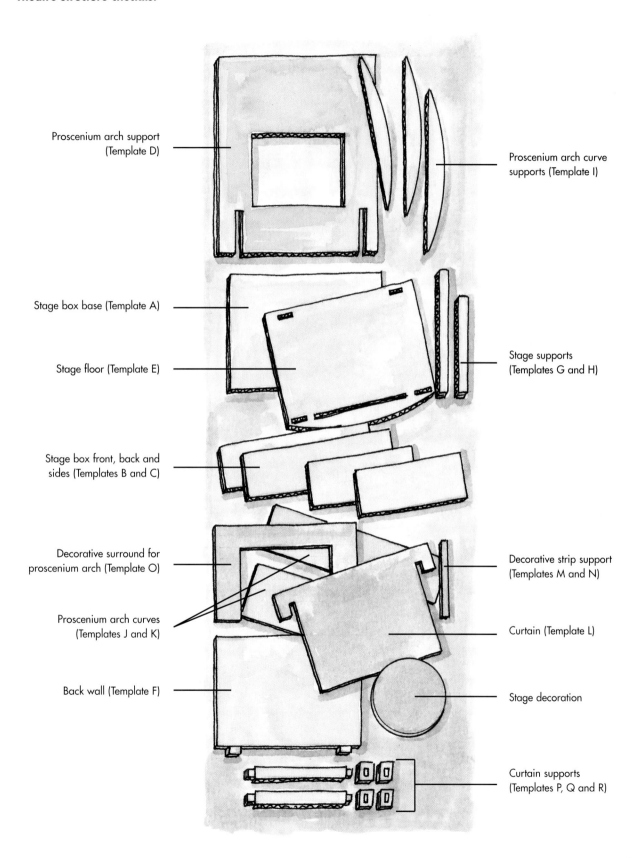

Proscenium arch support (Template D)

Proscenium arch curve supports (Template I)

Stage box base (Template A)

Stage floor (Template E)

Stage supports (Templates G and H)

Stage box front, back and sides (Templates B and C)

Decorative surround for proscenium arch (Template O)

Decorative strip support (Templates M and N)

Proscenium arch curves (Templates J and K)

Curtain (Template L)

Back wall (Template F)

Stage decoration

Curtain supports (Templates P, Q and R)

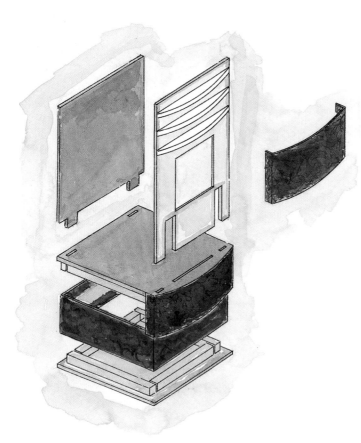

1 Colourwash the enlarged photocopies and backdrop with Prussian Blue ink.

2 Cut the long and short stage supports (Templates G and H) from corrugated card. Each support needs to be about ¾in (19mm) thick, so you may need to cut several layers and glue them together.

3 Cut the stage box base (Template A) and the stage floor (Template E) from corrugated card. Attach the stage supports to the stage box base and stage floor as shown in the diagram. Cut the stage box front and back (Template B) and the stage box sides (Template C). Construct the stage box using glued strips of paper to attach the pieces to each other so that they form a square (for more detailed advice see page 24). Cut a strip of corrugated card 17in x ½in (432mm x 13mm) and glue to the front of the square, so that it will run beneath the curve of the stage floor, acting as a support.

4 The stage box base, the square made from the front, back and sides and the stage floor should slot together without needing any adhesive, to create the theatre stage.

5 Cut the proscenium arch support (Template D) and back wall (Template F) from corrugated card. Fit the back wall into the slots at back of stage and proscenium arch into slots made at front of stage.

6 Cover all the exposed edges of card with strips of the colourwashed photocopy to give a neat and professional finish.

7 Cover the stage with blue colourwashed photocopy. Colourwash the decorative stage image with red watercolour and glaze it with a coat of PVA solution (one part glue to two parts water). Cut out the circular centre of the decorative stage image. Glue the four decorative corners taken from the circular stage image to the four corners of the stage.

8 Cover sides of the stage base box with crumpled purple and blue tissue paper. The easiest way of doing this is to cover the card with PVA or spray mount, and smooth the crumpled tissue with a firm hand until it is flat. This creates a beautiful deep colour over large expanses of material without the need for paints. It also gives a slightly marbled effect which can be emphasized by adding veins with a drawing pen and ink. Give the stage box a coat of PVA. Set the finished stage aside to dry.

9 Cut three proscenium arch curve supports (Template I) out of corrugated card. Cover the lower side of the bottom support and the upper side of the top support with blue colourwashed photocopy. Glue the supports to the top part of the proscenium arch and secure with small blocks of corrugated card.

10 Cover the back of the back wall with blue colourwashed photocopy and the front with the colourwashed backdrop. Cover or paint the tabs as well and glaze the whole piece with PVA solution (see Step 7).

11 Cut proscenium arch upper and lower curves (Templates J and K) out of flexible grey card. Cover both of these with blue and purple crumpled tissue paper, following the instructions in Step 8. Score these pieces where indicated and wrap around the proscenium arch, bending them gently into shape. Use dressmakers' pins to secure the pieces until the adhesive is dry. A clear contact adhesive is advisable for this job.

a

b

12 Cut the decorative surround for the proscenium arch (Template O) out of 500gsm white card. Cover the piece with orange and red tissue to create a marble effect. Finish off by drawing veins with gold ink to create a really plush effect. Seal this with PVA solution.

13 Mount the decorative pediment and pelmet images on to 500gsm white card and colour with blue and red watercolour inks. Also mount the red circular stage image (cut and painted in Step 7) on the same 500gsm card.

14 Take both sheets of acetate with drapes and cherubs image. Coat the tassels, cherubs and fringes with acrylic gold size. When the size is clear, after about 15 minutes, gild the size covered areas with Dutch gold leaf. Mount the two paper drapes and cherubs images onto the white paper copies. Cut them out and colour their whole area with red watercolour ink. Cut out the gold cherubs, tassels and fringes from the acetate and glue these to the red drapes so that the gilding is on the reverse side. Glue the drapes to the proscenium arch.

15 Cut four strips, the same size as the pediment image, out of 500gsm card. Glue to the reverse of the pediment image, then glue this to the proscenium arch. The blocks of card will help to create a three-dimensional effect.

16 Mount the pelmet image on 500gsm white card and emphasize the fabric shapes with fine gilding. Fix the pelmet image under the drapes, along the top edge of the proscenium opening. As in the previous step, small blocks of card, glued beneath the pelmet can be used to create a three-dimensional effect. Use small dabs of glue to secure the drapes to the pelmet.

17 Cut the two decorative strip supports (Templates M and N) out of 500gsm card. Cover the strips with orange tissue paper. The gold leaf scrolls were made on blue tissue paper using a rubber stamp (for more detailed instructions, see page 29). The scrolls were then torn out of the tissue paper in rough patches, and glued along the decorative strips.

18 Mount the photocopied scrolls onto card and paint with some red and blue watercolour ink mixed to make a purple colour. Finish the black lettering with some gold ink and a light spray of gold paint. Glue the large scroll to the top and the small scroll to the bottom of theatre, and affix the shield, gilded on the reverse, to the small scroll at the bottom.

19 Fix a small block of corrugated card to the bottom of the circular stage, so that it will be raised from the stage floor. Cut out the scenery image and mount it on to 500gsm white card and cut away the excess to create a three-dimensional effect. Fold the image into a curve and place it behind the circular stage.

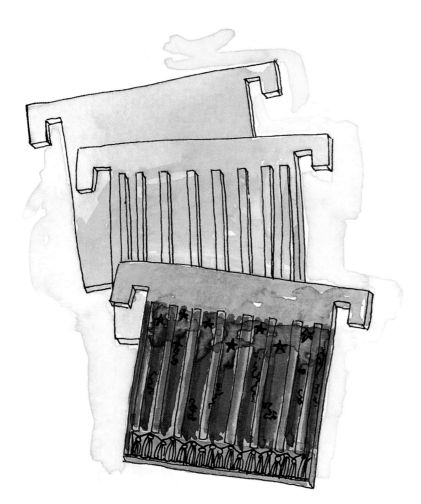

20 Cut the curtain shape (Template L) from 500gsm card. Cover the edges and the reverse side of the curtain with blue colourwashed photocopy. Glue strips of card to the curtain, these will create a draped effect. Cover the curtain with crumpled blue and purple tissue paper. Draw a simple rope and fringe image on red card with black ink. Finish with touches of gold pen or gilding. Glue curtain fringe image to bottom edge of curtain.

21 Cut the curtain support (Templates P and Q) and the curtain support receptors (Template R) from corrugated card. Glue four of each of the curtain support receptors together to make a four-ply piece. Fix the curtain support receptors to the back wall and reverse of the proscenium arch so that the curtain support can be hung between the two.

22 Mount the characters on 500gsm card, colour them with watercolours and inks and cut them out. Cut a small stand for each character out of corrugated card. Cover the stands with blue tissue paper or blue colourwashed paper and attach the characters to it. Your characters are now ready to take their places on the stage.

PART III

TEMPLATES AND DECORATIVE EFFECTS

DECORATIVE PHOTOCOPIES

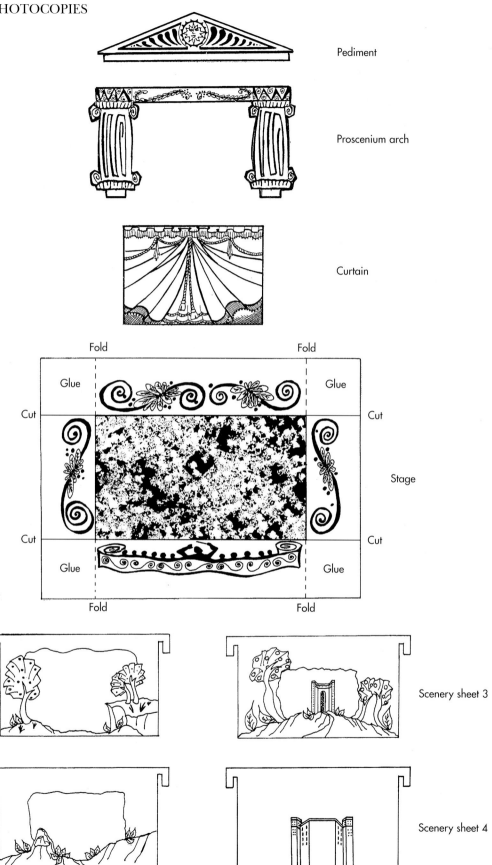

Pediment

Proscenium arch

Curtain

Stage

Scenery sheet 1

Scenery sheet 2

Scenery sheet 3

Scenery sheet 4

THEATRE IN A MATCHBOX

These images need to be enlarged by 200% using a photocopier

DECORATIVE PHOTOCOPIES

Music image

These images need to be enlarged by 200% using a photocopier

THEATRE STRUCTURE TEMPLATES

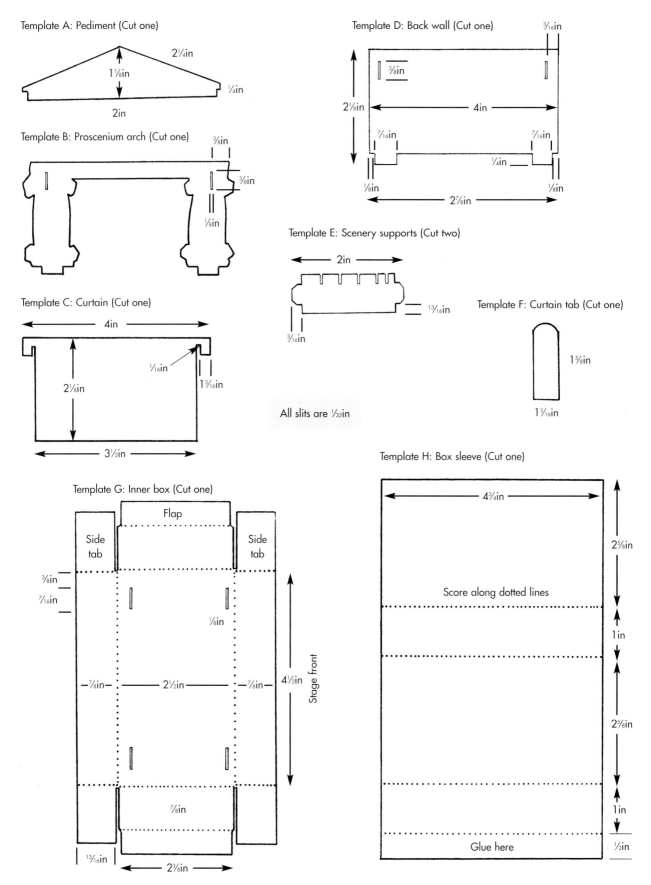

Template A: Pediment (Cut one)

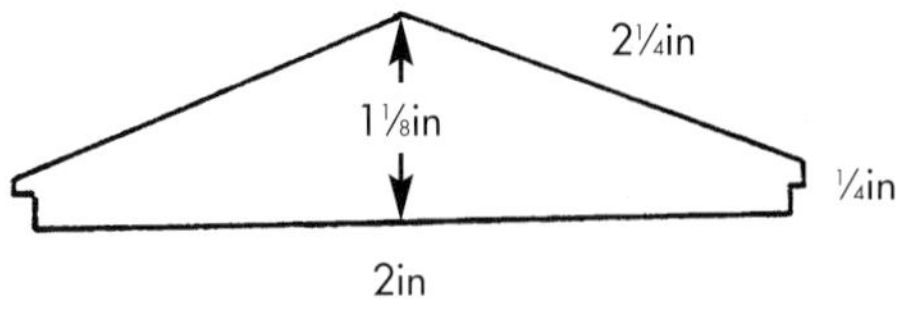
2¼in
1⅛in
¼in
2in

Template B: Proscenium arch (Cut one)

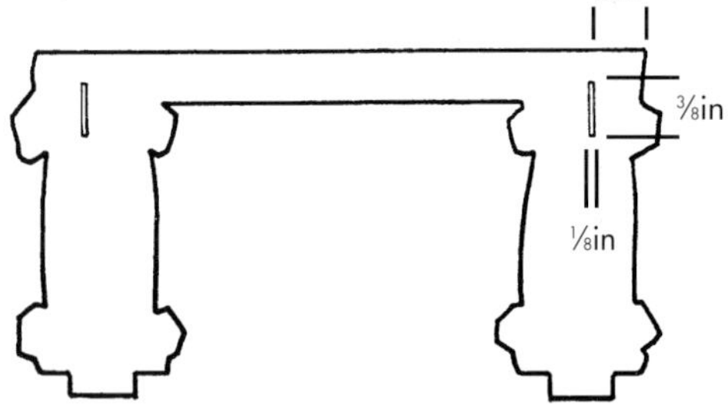
⅜in
⅜in
⅛in

Template C: Curtain (Cut one)

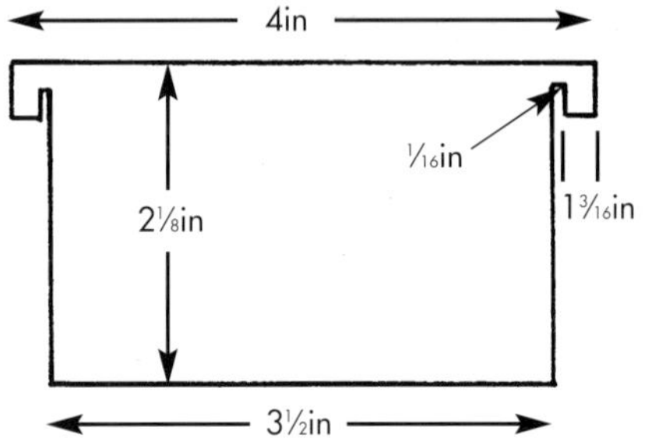
4in
1/16in
2⅛in
1 3/16in
3½in

Template D: Back wall (Cut one)

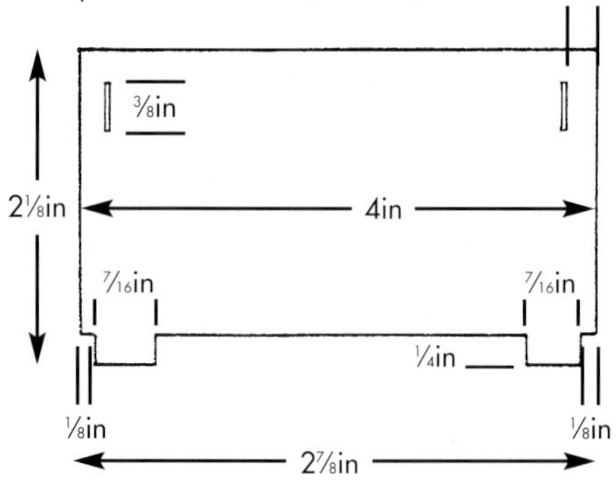
3/16in
⅜in
2⅛in
4in
7/16in
7/16in
¼in
⅛in
⅛in
2⅞in

Template E: Scenery supports (Cut two)

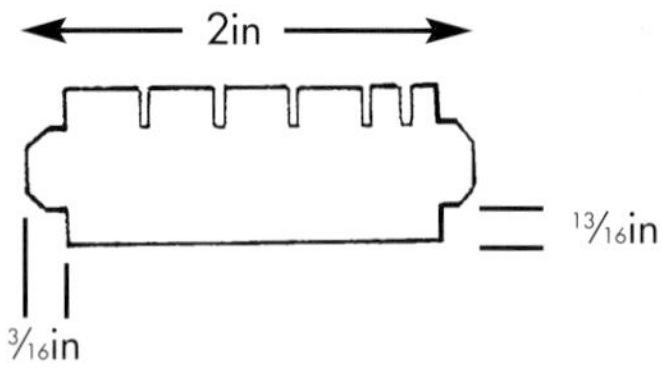
2in
13/16in
3/16in

Template F: Curtain tab (Cut one)

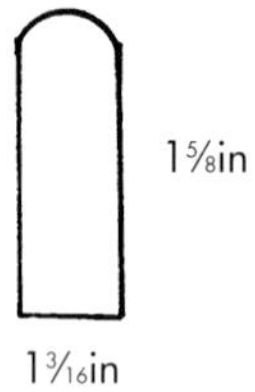
1⅝in
1 3/16in

All slits are 1/32in

Template G: Inner box (Cut one)

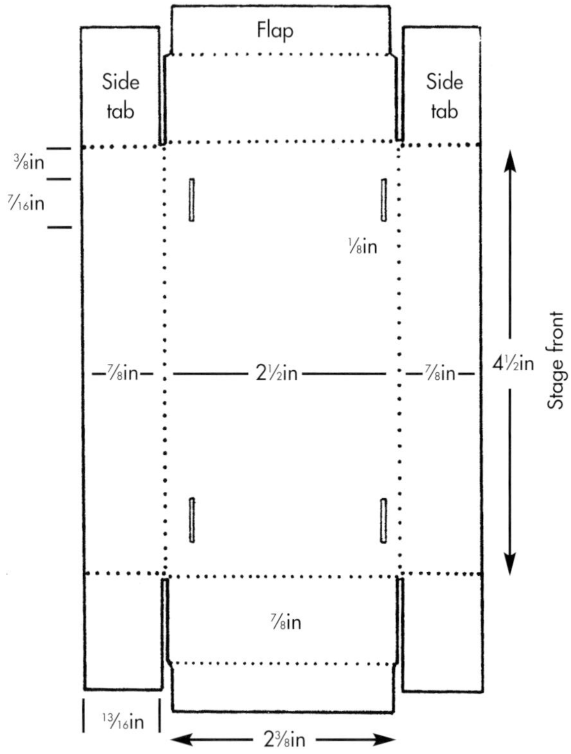
Flap
Side tab
Side tab
⅜in
7/16in
⅛in
⅞in
2½in
⅞in
4½in
Stage front
⅞in
13/16in
2⅜in

Template H: Box sleeve (Cut one)

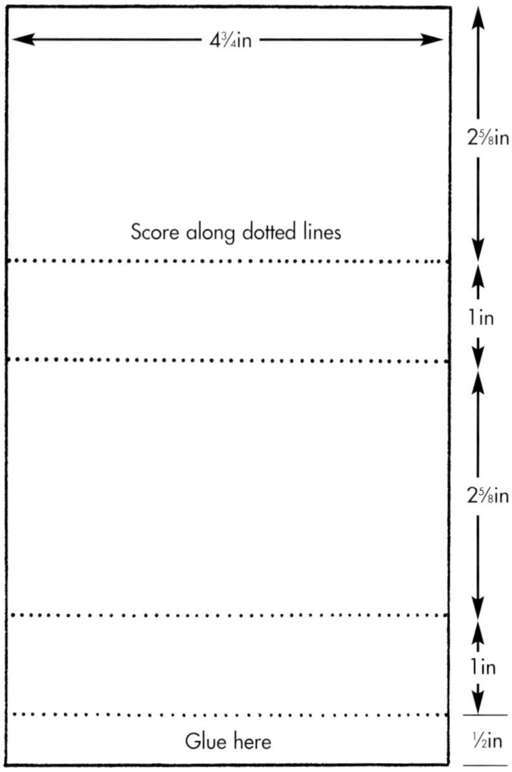
4¾in
2⅝in
Score along dotted lines
1in
2⅝in
1in
½in
Glue here

These templates need to be drawn using the dimensions given

DECORATIVE PHOTOCOPIES

Proscenium arch

Scenery image

FOLDING THEATRE IN A BOX

These images need to be enlarged by 200% using a photocopier

THEATRE STRUCTURE TEMPLATES

FOLDING THEATRE IN A BOX

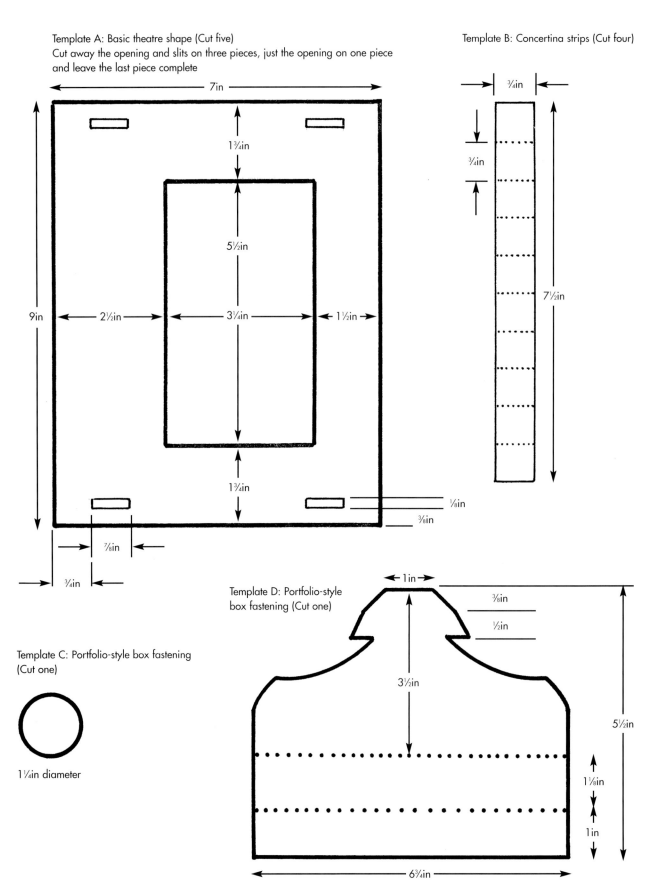

Template A: Basic theatre shape (Cut five)
Cut away the opening and slits on three pieces, just the opening on one piece and leave the last piece complete

7in

9in

1¾in

5½in

2½in   3¼in   1½in

1¾in

⅛in

⅜in

⅞in

¾in

Template B: Concertina strips (Cut four)

¾in

¾in

7½in

Template C: Portfolio-style box fastening (Cut one)

1¼in diameter

Template D: Portfolio-style box fastening (Cut one)

1in

⅜in

½in

3½in

5½in

1⅛in

1in

6¾in

These templates need to be drawn using the dimensions given

Theatre structure templates

Template E: Portfolio-style box (Cut one)

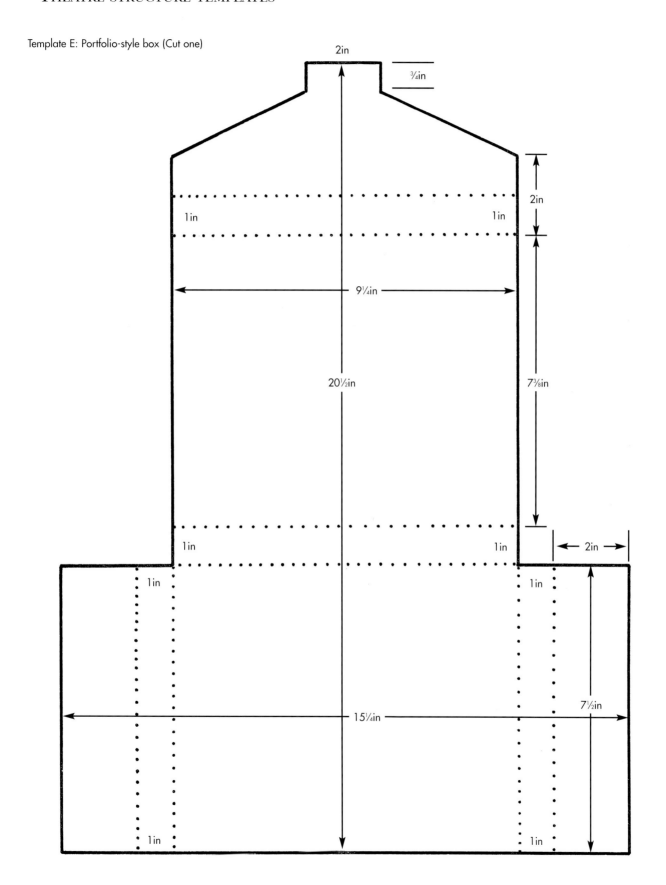

These templates need to be drawn using the dimensions given

Decorative photocopies

Proscenium arch

Scenery image 1

Scenery image 2

110

These images need to be enlarged by 200% using a photocopier

DECORATIVE PHOTOCOPIES

Scenery image 3

Backdrop

Curtain image 1

Curtain image 2

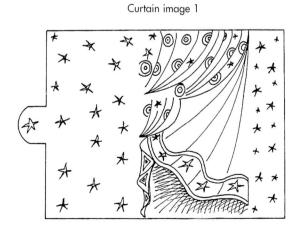

These images need to be enlarged by 200% using a photocopier

Theatre structure templates

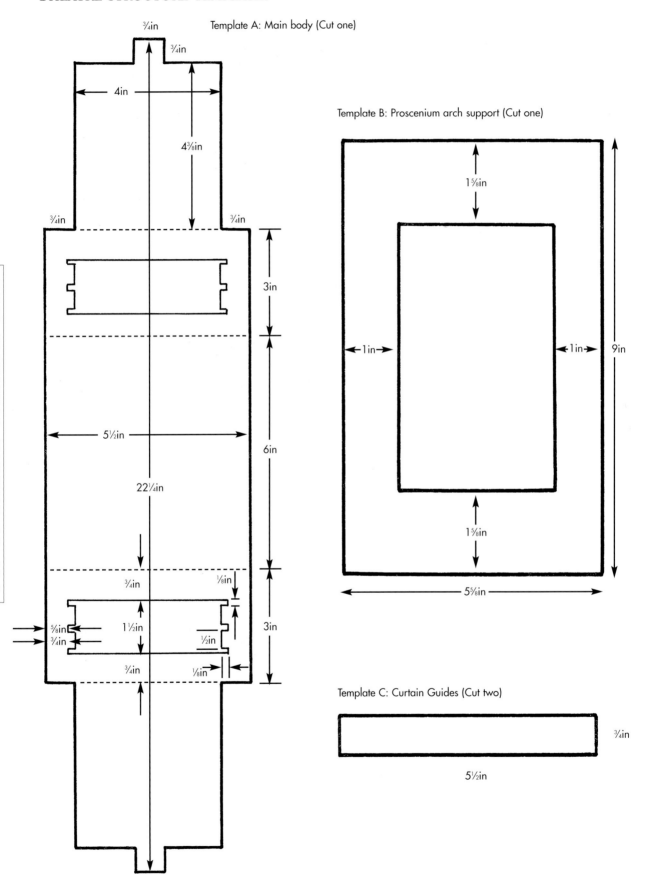

Template A: Main body (Cut one)

¾in

¾in

4in

4⅜in

¾in   ¾in

3in

5½in   6in

22¼in

¾in   ⅛in

⅝in
¾in   1½in   ½in

¾in   ⅛in   3in

Template B: Proscenium arch support (Cut one)

1⅝in

1in→   ←1in   9in

1⅝in

5⅝in

Template C: Curtain Guides (Cut two)

¾in

5½in

These templates need to be drawn using the dimensions given

DECORATIVE PHOTOCOPIES

Curtain

Proscenium arch

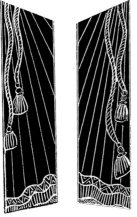

Curtain wings

Box label

Backdrop

Characters x 4

Scenery wings x 4

These images need to be enlarged by 200% using a photocopier

THEATRE STRUCTURE TEMPLATES

Template A: Top theatre base (Cut one)

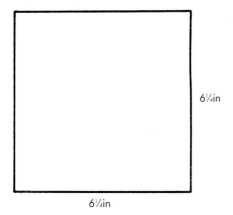

6¼in

6¼in

Template B: Middle theatre base (Cut one)

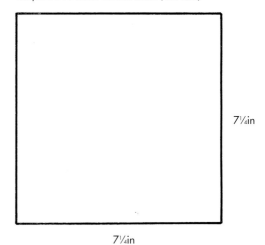

7¼in

7¼in

Template C: Lower theatre base (Cut one)

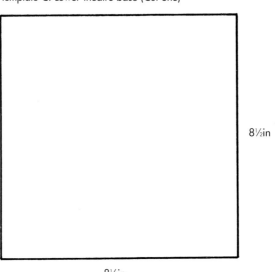

8½in

8½in

Templates for front and rear boxes

Template D: Rear box – front and back (Cut two)

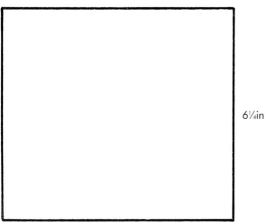

6¼in

7⅛in

Template E: Front box – proscenium arch (Cut two)

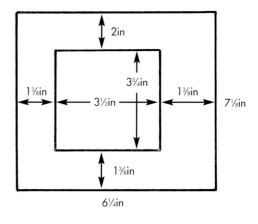

2in

1⅜in   3½in   3¾in   1⅜in   7⅛in

1⅜in

6¼in

OPERA HOUSE

These templates need to be drawn using the dimensions given

THEATRE STRUCTURE TEMPLATES

Template F: Sides of both front and rear box (Cut four)

7⅛in   1¼in

Template G: Top and bottom of front and rear box (Cut four)

6⅜in   1¼in

Template H: Proscenium arch – inner surround (Cut two)

1¼in   3⅝in

Template I: Proscenium arch – inner surround (Cut two)

1¼in   3¼in

Template J: Stage support (Cut two)

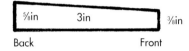

⅝in   3in   ⅜in

Back   Front

Stage templates

Template K: Upper stage layer (Cut one)

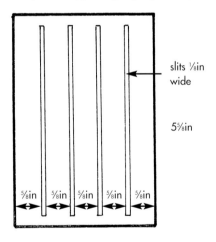

slits ⅛in wide

5⅝in

⅝in ⅝in ⅝in ⅝in ⅝in

Template L: Stage base (Cut one)

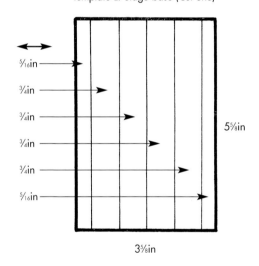

5/16in
¾in
¾in
¾in
¾in
5/16in

5⅝in

3⅝in

Template M: Character guide and sides of stage (Cut seven)

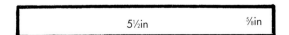

5½in   ⅝in

Template N: Stage side (Cut one)

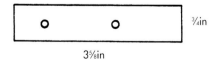

¾in

3⅝in

Template O: Stage side (Cut one)

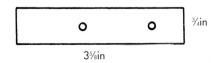

¾in

3⅝in

OPERA HOUSE

These templates need to be drawn using the dimensions given

Theatre structure templates

Template P: Curtain tab (Cut one)

Template Q: Curtain (Cut one)

Template R: Curtain guide
(Cut two)

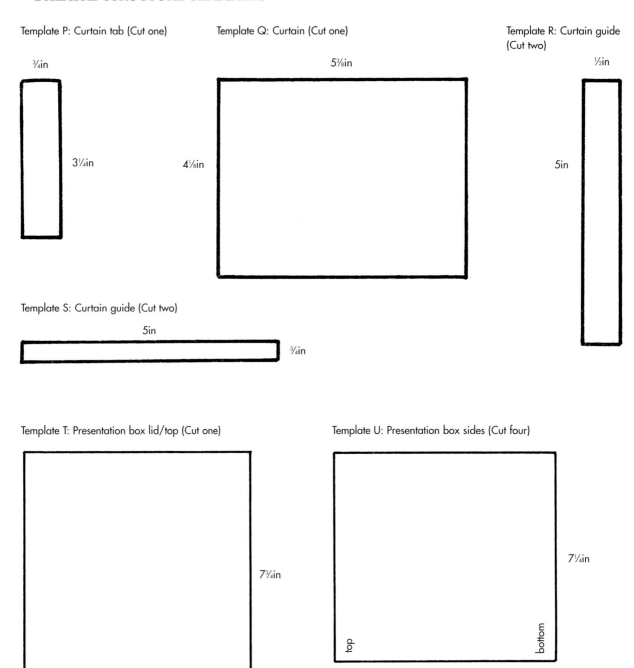

¾in

3¼in

5⅜in

4⅛in

½in

5in

Template S: Curtain guide (Cut two)

5in

¾in

Template T: Presentation box lid/top (Cut one)

7¾in

7¾in

Template U: Presentation box sides (Cut four)

7¼in

top

bottom

7¾in

These templates need to be drawn using the dimensions given

Decorative photocopies

Scenery image

Decorative image for covering box

Crown decoration - This template needs to be enlarged by 273% using a photocopier

These images need to be enlarged by 200% using a photocopier

THEATRE STRUCTURE TEMPLATES
Templates for theatre box

Template A: Back of box (Cut one)

Template B: Top and bottom of box (Cut two and remove the centre of one to form the top of the box)

Template C: Sides of box (Cut two)

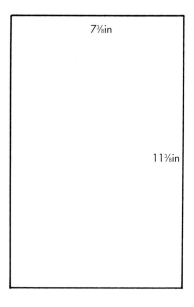

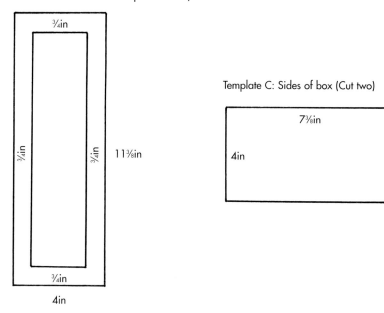

Template D: Proscenium frame base (Cut three and glue together)

Template E: Proscenium frame (Cut one)

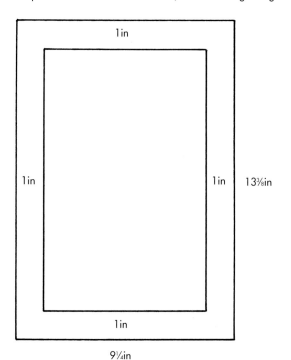

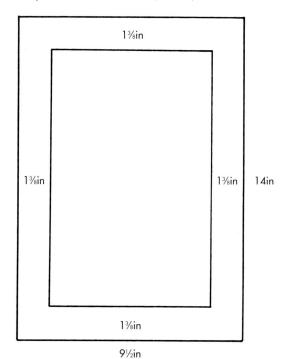

THREE-DIMENSIONAL THEATRE PICTURE

These templates need to be drawn using the dimensions given

DECORATIVE PHOTOCOPIES

Balcony box

Conductor and
orchestra

Small audience
images

Moose

Deer and trees scenery

Stars

Moons

Large audience

Tree 1

Tree 2

WINTER WONDERLAND

These images need to be enlarged by 200% using a photocopier

Decorative photocopies

Winter Wonderland

Proscenium arch

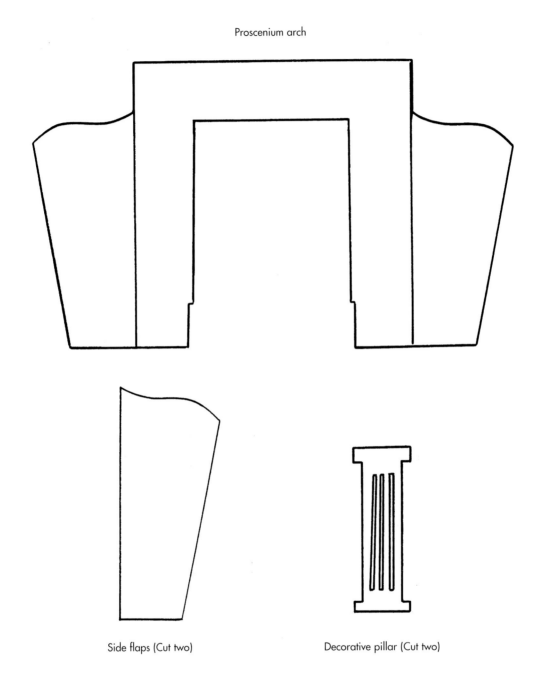

Side flaps (Cut two)

Decorative pillar (Cut two)

These images need to be enlarged by 200% using a photocopier

DECORATIVE PHOTOCOPIES

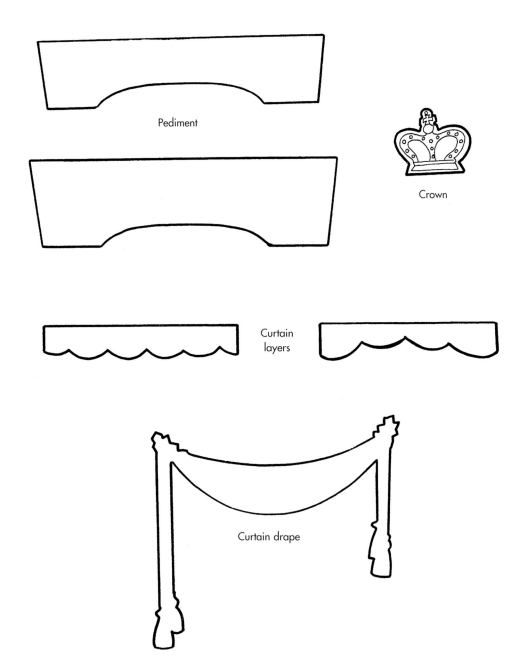

Pediment

Crown

Curtain
layers

Curtain drape

These images need to be enlarged by 200% using a photocopier

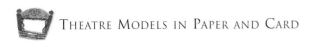

THEATRE STRUCTURE TEMPLATES

Theatre base and stage templates

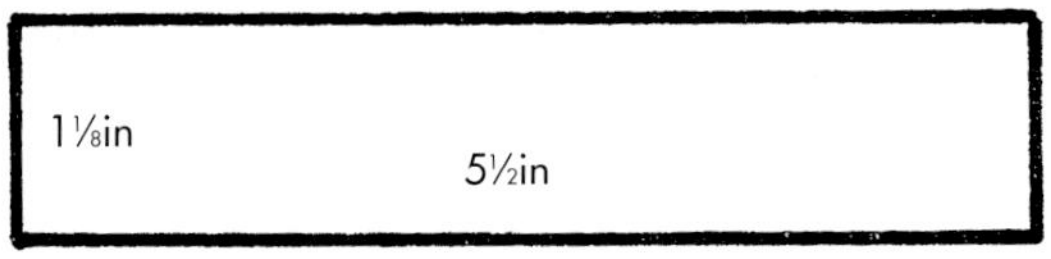
1⅛in
5½in

Template A: Stage back (Cut one)

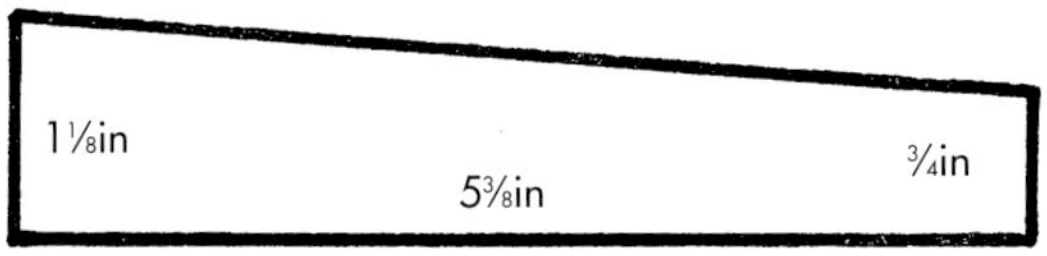
1⅛in
5⅜in
¾in

Template B: Stage sides (Cut two)

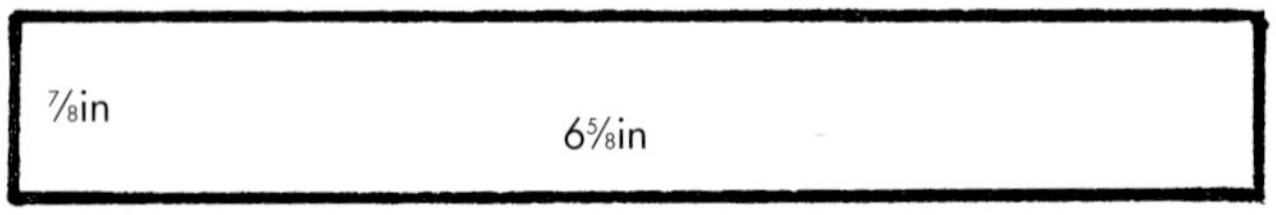
⅞in
6⅝in

Template C: Stage front (Cut one)

Template D: Stage base (Cut one)

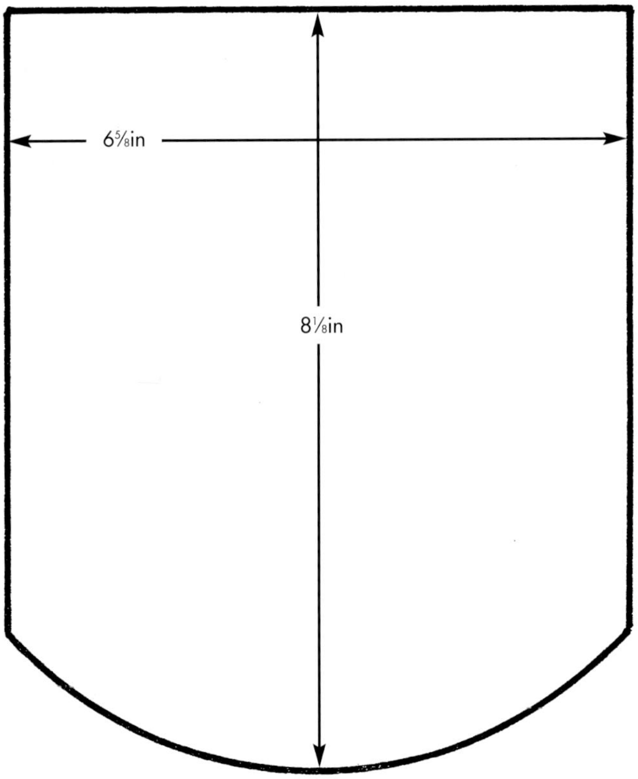
6⅝in
8⅛in

Template E: Upper stage layer (Cut one)

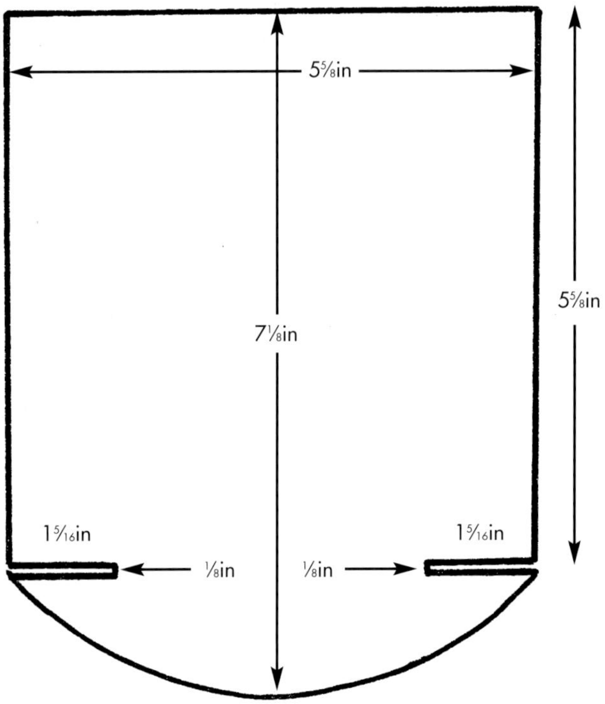
5⅝in
7⅛in
5⅝in
1 5/16in
1 5/16in
⅛in
⅛in

These templates need to be drawn using the dimensions given

THEATRE STRUCTURE TEMPLATES
Theatre base and stage templates

Template F: Back wall (Cut one)

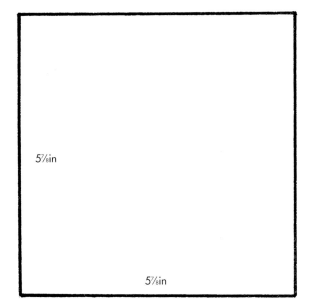

Template G: Theatre sides (Cut two and cut each in half)

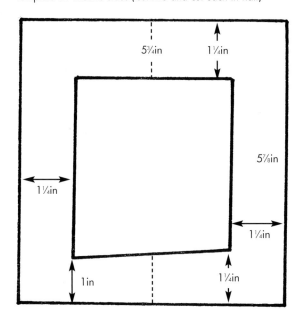

Template H: Proscenium arch support (Cut one)

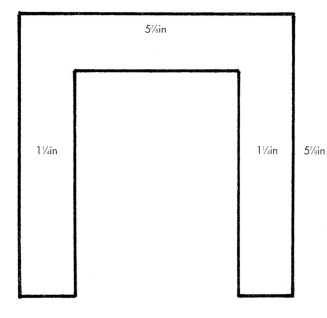

Template I: Curtain (Cut one)

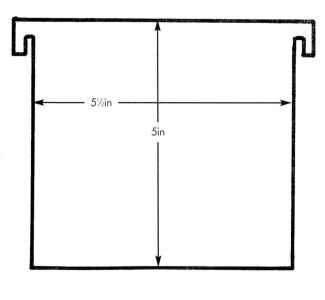

WINTER WONDERLAND

Theatre structure templates
Templates for box base

Template J: Box base inserts (Cut one) Template K: Box base sides (Cut two) Template L: Box base ends (Cut two)

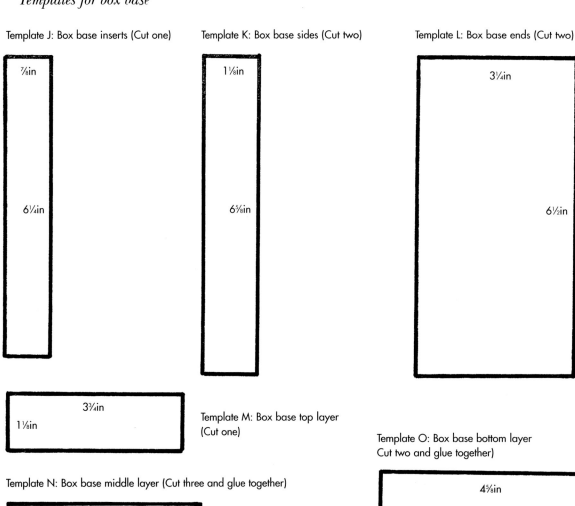

⅞in

6¼in

1⅛in

6⅝in

3¼in

6½in

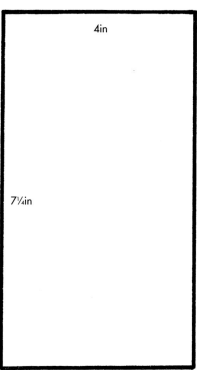

3¾in

1⅛in

Template M: Box base top layer
(Cut one)

Template N: Box base middle layer (Cut three and glue together)

4in

7¼in

Template O: Box base bottom layer
Cut two and glue together)

4⅝in

8in

These templates need to be drawn using the dimensions given

WINTER WONDERLAND

THEATRE STRUCTURE TEMPLATES
Presentation box templates

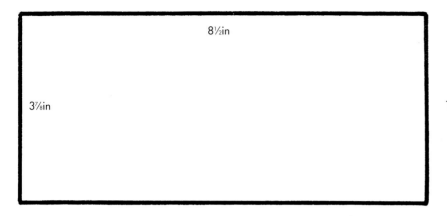

Template P: Box sides (Cut two)

Template Q: Box top (Cut one)

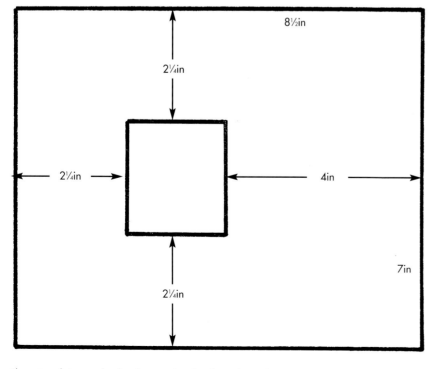

Template R: Box front and back
(Cut two and remove window from one)

These templates need to be drawn using the dimensions given

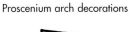

Decorative photocopies

Proscenium arch decorations

Four characters

Curtain

These images need to be enlarged by 200% using a photocopier

DECORATIVE PHOTOCOPIES

Character decoration for base

Scenery image 1

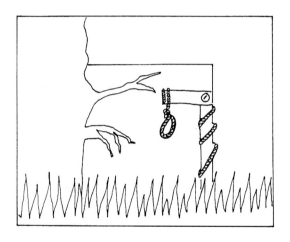

Scenery image 2

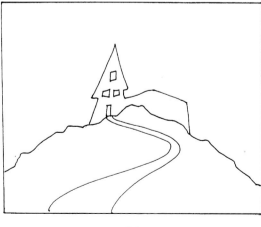

Backdrop

These images need to be enlarged by 200% using a photocopier

THEATRE STRUCTURE TEMPLATES

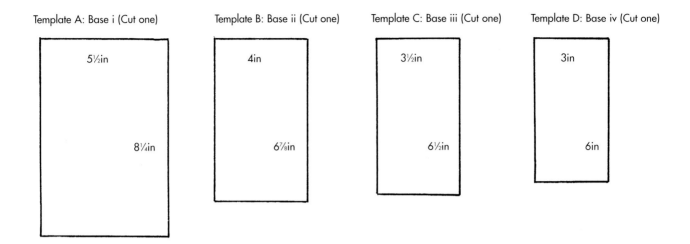

Template A: Base i (Cut one)

5½in

8¼in

Template B: Base ii (Cut one)

4in

6⅞in

Template C: Base iii (Cut one)

3½in

6½in

Template D: Base iv (Cut one)

3in

6in

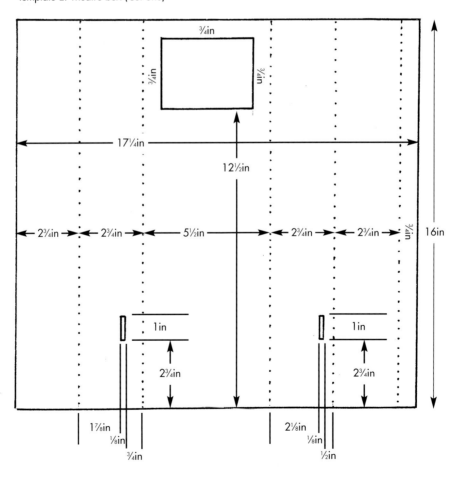

Template E: Theatre box (Cut one)

¾in

¾in ¾in

17¼in

12½in

2¾in ← 2¾in → 5½in ← 2¾in → 2¾in

¾in

16in

1in

2¾in

1in

2¾in

1⅞in

⅛in

¾in

2⅛in

⅛in

½in

These templates need to be drawn using the dimensions given

THEATRE STRUCTURE TEMPLATES

Template G: Lever (Cut four)

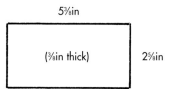

10¼in

½in

Template H: Lever handle (Cut two)

6½in

½in

Template F: Inside support for movement (Cut two)

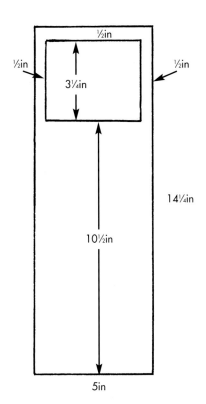

½in

½in

3¼in

½in

14¼in

10½in

5in

Template I: Inside movement base (Cut three)

5⅜in

(⅜in thick)

2⅝in

Template J: Inside movement strut (Cut four)

5⅜in

1¼in

Template K: Proscenium arch surround side (Cut two)

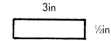

3in

½in

Template L: Proscenium arch surround bottom (Cut one)

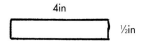

4in

½in

Template M: Top of booth (Cut one)

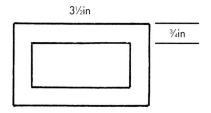

3½in

¾in

These templates need to be drawn using the dimensions given

DECORATIVE PHOTOCOPIES

VICTORIAN THEATRE ROYALE

Proscenium arch decoration

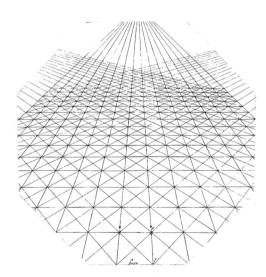

Perspective stage decoration

Characters

Theatre Royale

Presentation box label

These images need to be enlarged by 200% using a photocopier

DECORATIVE PHOTOCOPIES

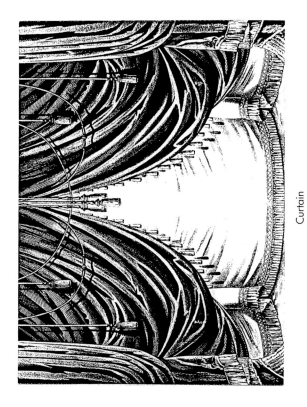

Curtain

Scenery wing 3

Scenery wing 2

Scenery wing 1

Scenery image

Backdrop

VICTORIAN THEATRE ROYALE

These images need to be enlarged by 200% using a photocopier

Theatre structure templates

Template A: Proscenium arch support (Cut one)

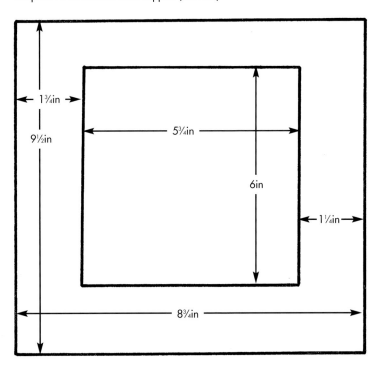

1¾in

9½in

5¾in

6in

1¼in

8¾in

Template B: Back wall (Cut one)

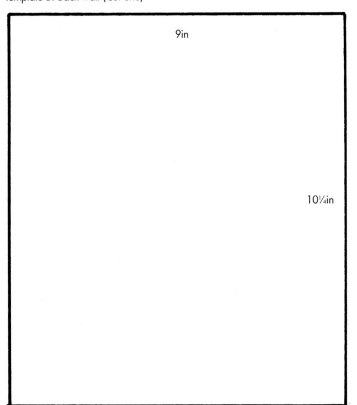

9in

10¼in

Template C: Scenery support receptor
(Cut eight)

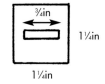

¾in

1¼in

1¼in

Template D: Stage support receptor
(Cut eight)

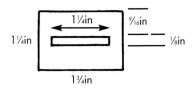

1¼in

⁵⁄₁₆in

1¼in

⅛in

1¾in

These templates need to be drawn using the dimensions given

THEATRE STRUCTURE TEMPLATES

Template E: Stage support (Cut four)

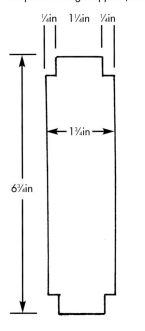

Template G: Curtain guide inner (Cut one)

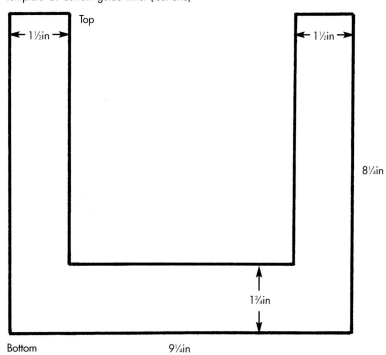

Template F: Scenery support (Cut four)

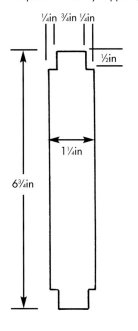

Template H: Curtain guide outer (Cut one)

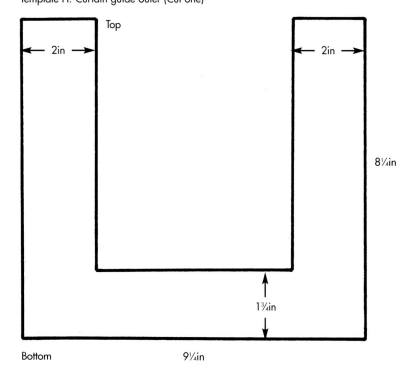

These templates need to be drawn using the dimensions given

THEATRE STRUCTURE TEMPLATES

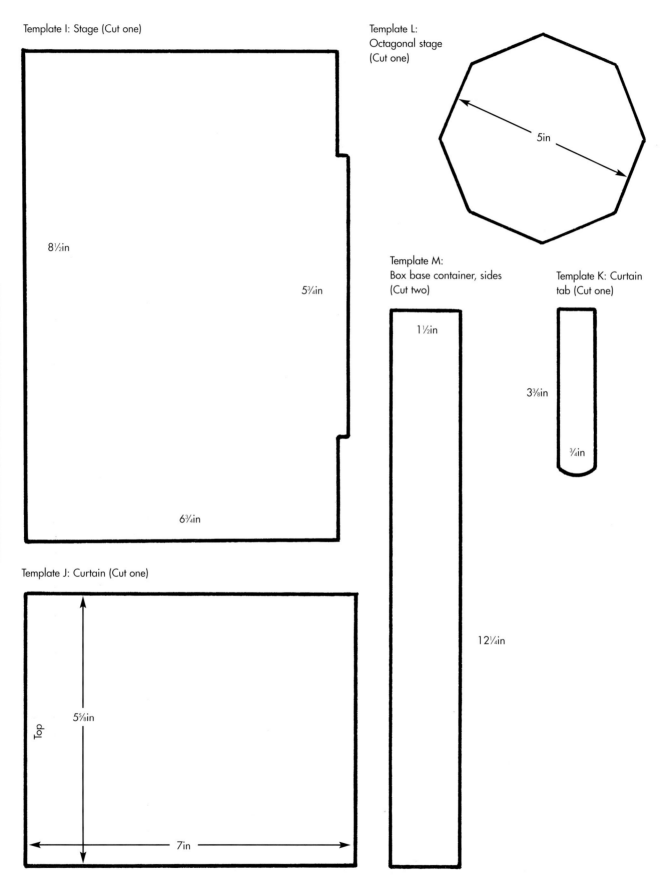

Template I: Stage (Cut one)

8½in

5¾in

6¾in

Victorian Theatre Royale

Template J: Curtain (Cut one)

Top

5⅝in

7in

Template L:
Octagonal stage
(Cut one)

5in

Template M:
Box base container, sides
(Cut two)

1½in

12¼in

Template K: Curtain
tab (Cut one)

3⅜in

¾in

These templates need to be drawn using the dimensions given

Theatre structure templates

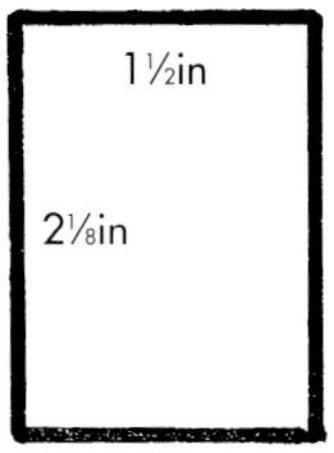

Template N:
Box base container, ends
(Cut two)

1½in

2⅛in

Template O: Box top, bottom
(Cut one)

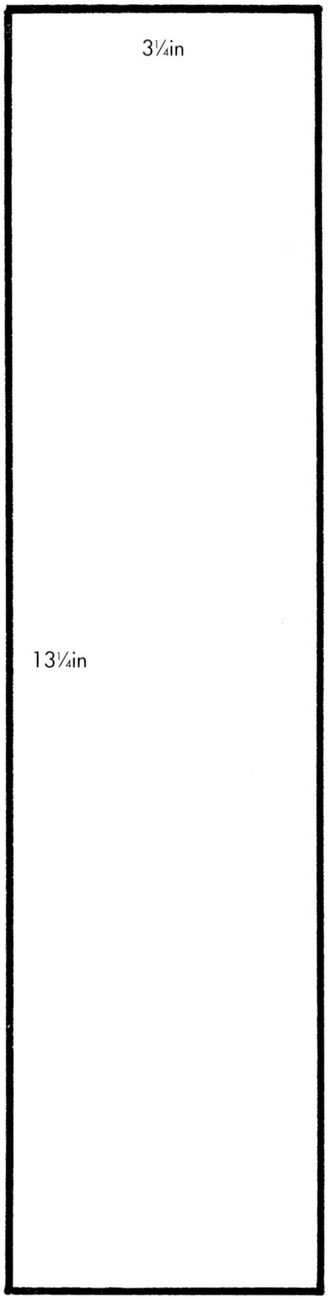

3¼in

13¼in

Template P: Box top,
middle (Cut one)

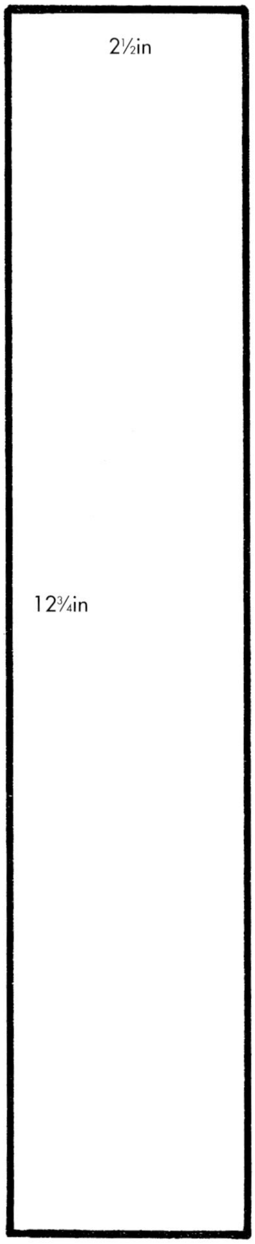

2½in

12¾in

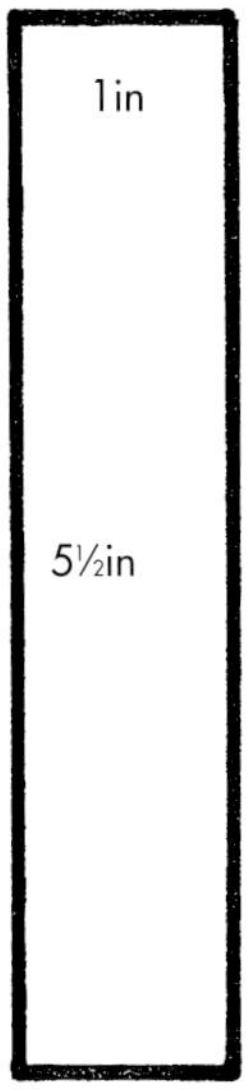

Template R: Box top base
(Cut two)

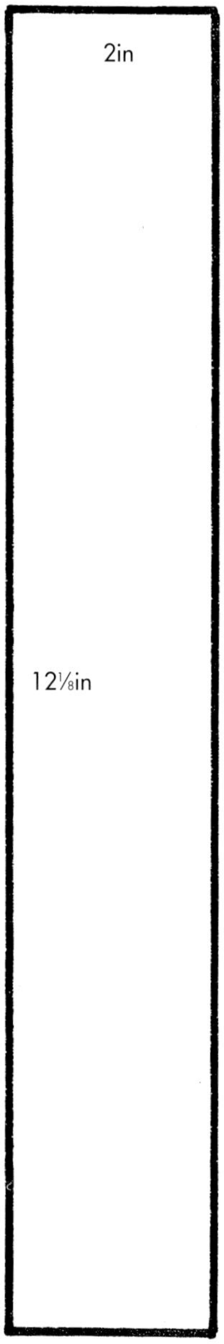

2in

12⅛in

Template Q:
Handle base
(Cut four and
glue together)

1in

5½in

These templates need to be drawn using the dimensions given

Theatre structure templates

Template S: Box middle
base (Cut one)

3½in

13⅝in

Template T: Box bottom
base (Cut one)

4in

14⅛in

Template U: Scenery support sheet (Cut four)

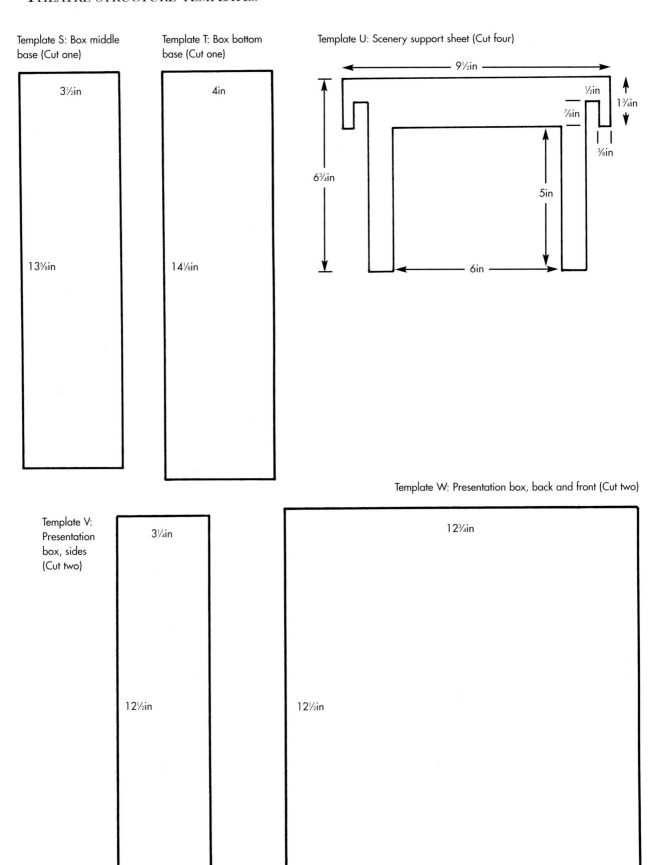

9½in

6¾in

5in

6in

½in

⅞in

1¾in

⅜in

Template V:
Presentation
box, sides
(Cut two)

3¼in

12½in

Template W: Presentation box, back and front (Cut two)

12¾in

12½in

These templates need to be drawn using the dimensions given

Decorative photocopies

Sliding screen 1

Characters

Sliding screen 2

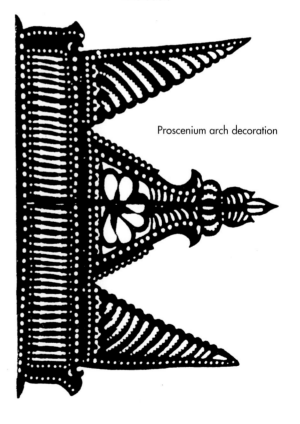

Proscenium arch decoration

Lower edge of proscenium arch

These images need to be enlarged by 400% using a photocopier,
except for the characters which need to be enlarged by 200%

Theatre structure templates

Template A: Proscenium arch support (Cut three)

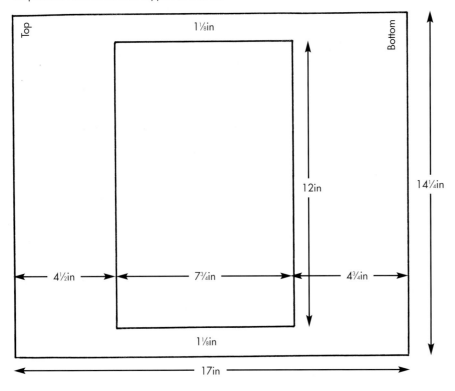

Top

Bottom

1⅛in

12in

14¼in

4½in

7¾in

4¾in

1⅛in

17in

Template B:
Stand base
(Cut three)

Template C:
Front edge support
(Cut one)

Template D:
Back edge support
(Cut three)

Template E:
Screen guide, inner
(Cut six)

Template F:
Screen guide, outer
(Cut four)

Template G:
Stand support
(Cut eight)

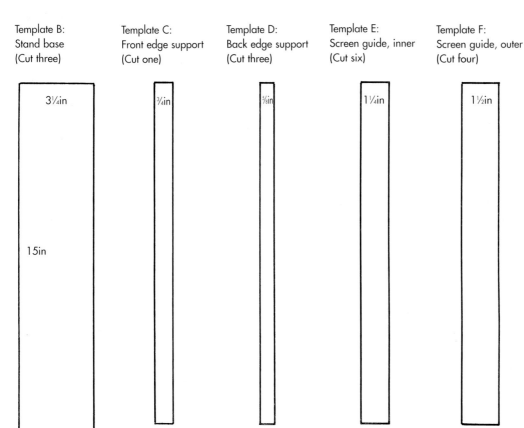

3¼in

15in

¾in

⅝in

1¼in

1½in

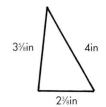

3⅝in

4in

2⅜in

These templates need to be drawn using the dimensions given

Decorative photocopies

Shield image

Large scroll image

Curtain decoration 1

Stage decoration

Decorative scroll image

These images need to be enlarged by 200% using a photocopier

Decorative photocopies

Shield scroll

Curtain
decoration 2

Use for enlarging
and covering

Backdrop and
covering image

These images need to be enlarged by 200% using a photocopier

DECORATIVE PHOTOCOPIES

Pelmet

Pediment image

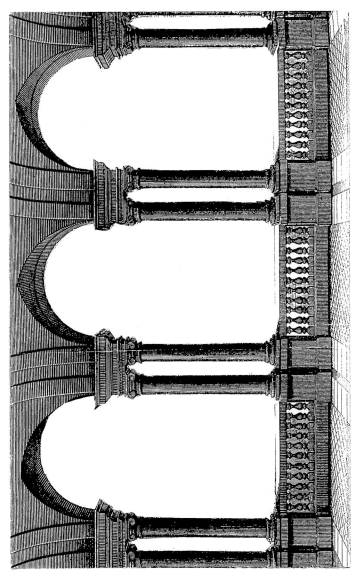

Scenery image

Characters

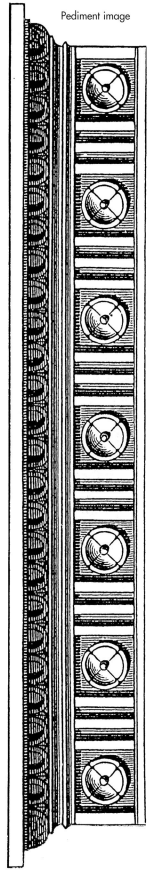

THEATRE GRANDE

These images need to be enlarged by 200% using a photocopier

THEATRE STRUCTURE TEMPLATES

Template A: Stage box base (Cut one)

Template B: Stage box front and back
(Cut two)

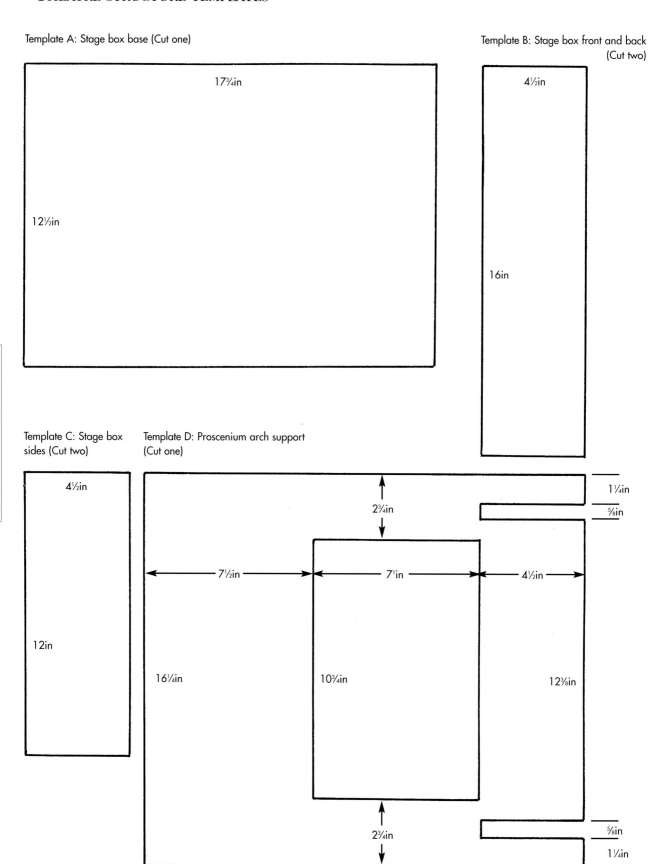

Template C: Stage box
sides (Cut two)

Template D: Proscenium arch support
(Cut one)

THEATRE GRANDE

These templates need to be drawn using the dimensions given.

THEATRE STRUCTURE TEMPLATES

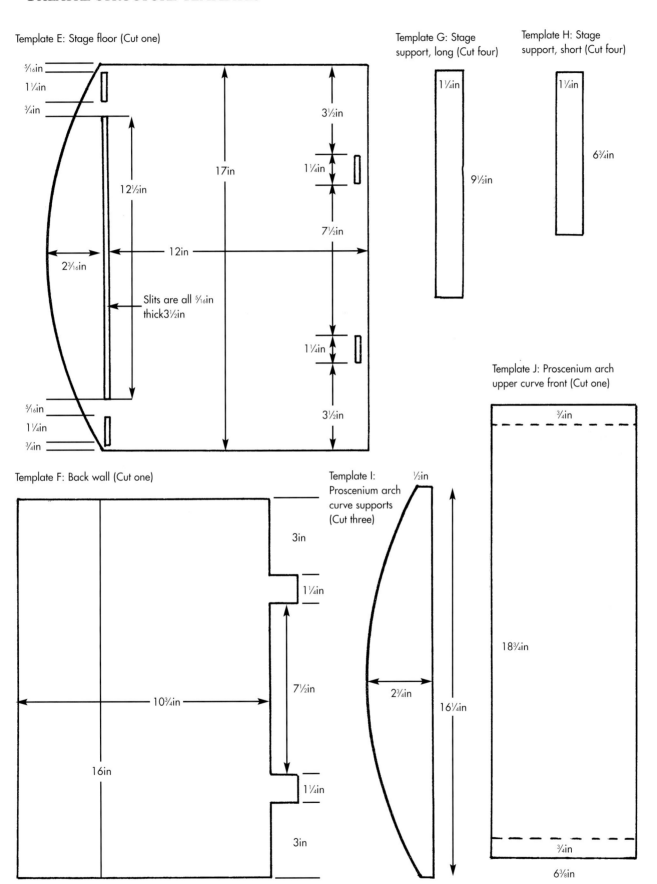

Template E: Stage floor (Cut one)

⁵⁄₁₆in
1¼in
¾in

3½in

17in

1¼in

12½in

7½in

12in

2³⁄₁₆in

Slits are all ⁵⁄₁₆in thick3½in

1¼in

⁵⁄₁₆in
1¼in
¾in

3½in

Template G: Stage support, long (Cut four)

1¼in

9½in

Template H: Stage support, short (Cut four)

1¼in

6¾in

Template F: Back wall (Cut one)

3in

1¼in

7½in

10¾in

16in

1¼in

3in

Template I: Proscenium arch curve supports (Cut three)

½in

2¾in

16¼in

Template J: Proscenium arch upper curve front (Cut one)

¾in

18¾in

¾in

6⅜in

These templates need to be drawn using the dimensions given.

THEATRE STRUCTURE TEMPLATES

Template K: Proscenium arch lower front curve (Cut one)

Template L: Curtain (Cut one)

Template M: Decorative strip support, upper (Cut one)

Table N: Decorative strip support, lower (Cut one)

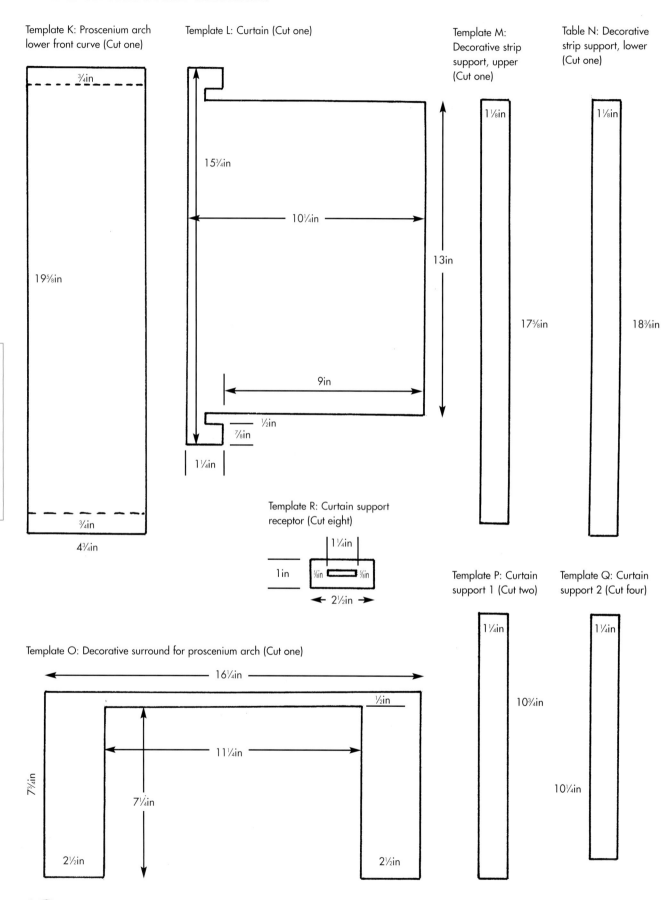

THEATRE GRANDE

Template R: Curtain support receptor (Cut eight)

Template P: Curtain support 1 (Cut two)

Template Q: Curtain support 2 (Cut four)

Template O: Decorative surround for proscenium arch (Cut one)

These templates need to be drawn using the dimensions given

PART IV

RESOURCES

Measurement Conversion Table

Inches to millimetres and centimetres

inches	mm	cm	inches	cm	inches	cm
⅛	3	0.3	9	22.9	30	76.2
¼	6	0.6	10	25.4	31	78.7
⅜	10	1.0	11	27.9	32	81.3
½	13	1.3	12	30.5	33	83.8
⅝	16	1.6	13	33.0	34	86.4
¾	19	1.9	14	35.6	35	88.9
⅞	22	2.2	15	38.1	36	91.4
1	25	2.5	16	40.6	37	94.0
1¼	32	3.2	17	43.2	38	96.5
1½	38	3.8	18	45.7	39	99.1
1¾	44	4.4	19	48.3	40	101.6
2	51	5.1	20	50.8	41	104.1
2½	64	6.4	21	53.3	42	106.7
3	76	7.6	22	55.9	43	109.2
3½	89	8.9	23	58.4	44	111.8
4	102	10.2	24	61.0	45	114.3
4½	114	11.4	25	63.5	46	116.8
5	127	12.7	26	66.0	47	119.4
6	152	15.2	27	68.6	48	121.9
7	178	17.8	28	71.1	49	124.5
8	203	20.3	29	73.7	50	127.0

Although care has been taken to ensure metric measurements are true and accurate, they are only conversions from imperial. The template dimensions are given in imperial measurements only, to ensure consistency.

LIST OF SUPPLIERS

UNITED KINGDOM

General

Fred Aldous Ltd *
PO Box 135
37 Lever Street
Manchester
M60 1UX
Tel: 0161 236 2477
Fax: 0161 236 6075
email: Aldous@btinternet.com

Craft Creations Ltd *
Ingersoll House
Delamare Road
Chestnut
Hertfordshire
EN8 9ND
Tel: 01992 781900
Fax: 01992 634339
email: enquries@craftcreations.
com
website: www.craftcreations.
com

Educational Art and Craft
Supplies Ltd*
17 Lisle Avenue
Kidderminster
Worcestershire
DY11 7DE
Tel: 01562 744 522
Fax: 01562 823181

Falkiner Fine Paper*
76 Southampton Row
London
WC1B 4AR
Tel: 0171 831 1151
Fax: 0171 430 1248

T. N. Lawrence and Son*
117–119 Clerkenwell Road
London
EC1R 5BY
Tel: 01273 488188
Fax: 0171 430 2234
email: Mlawrence@lawrence.
co.uk
website: www.lawrence. co.uk

London Graphic Centre*
Unit 9–10 Makay Trading Estate
Kensal Road
London
W10 5BN
Tel: 0171 240 0095
Fax: 0171 831 1554

Paperchase*
213 Tottenham Court Road
London
WIP 9AF
Tel: 0171 323 3707
Fax: 0171 637 1225
email: paperchase@
paperchase.telme.com

E. Plutons*
273 Archway Road
London
N6 5AA
Tel: 0181 348 0315
Fax: 0181 348 3414
email: pluton@pluton.co.uk
website: www.pluton.co.uk/
pluton

Design sources

The Dover Bookshop*
18 Earlham Street
London
WC2
Tel: 0171 836 2111
Fax: 0171 836 1603
email: images@
thedoverbookshop.com

Toy theatre suppliers

Pollock's Toy Theatre
Museum*
1 Scala Street
London
W1P 1LT
Tel: 0171 636 3452
email: toytheatres@hotmail.
com

* Mail order available

SOUTH AFRICA

General
X - Press Graph - X*
29 Siemert Road
Doornfontein 2094
Tel: 011 402 4522
Fax: 011 402 4599

Crafty Supplies*
Shop 104
The Atrium
Main Road
Claremont
Cape Town 7708
Tel: 27 21 610286
Fax: 27 21 610308

U.S.A

General
All Craft Tool and Supply
Company Inc
666 Pacific St
Brooklyn
NY 11217-2109
Tel: 718 789 2800

Art Supply Warehouse Inc
360 Main Ave
Norwalk
CT 06851-1549
Tel: 203 846 2279

Art Shoppe
24625 Del Prado
Dana Point
CA 92629-2804
Tel: 714 488 8977
Fax: 714 493 6777

Creative Expressions
7240 Shadeland Station
Indianapolis
IN 46256
Tel: 800 428 5017

Daniel Smith Inc*
Fine Artists' Materials
PO Box 84268
Seattle
WA 98124-5568
Tel: 206 223 9599
Fax: 206 224 0404
email:dsartmtrl@aol.com

Kate's Paperie
561 Broadway
New York
NY 10012-3918
Tel: 212 941 9816

Paper Source
232 W Chicago Ave
Chicago
IL 60616-3107
Tel: 312 337 0798

Sam Flax
12 W 20th St
New York
NY 10011-4203
Tel: 212 620 3038

Sax Arts and Crafts
2405 S Calhoun Rd
New Berlin
WI 53151-2744
Tel: 414 784 6880

Toy theatre suppliers
The Toy Theatre Company*
12401 Cambridge Boulevard
Ocean Springs
MS 39564
Tel: 228 875 3102
email: g_sndbrg@datasync.com

AUSTRALIA

General
Janet's Art Supplies and Books
Pty Ltd*
143 Victoria Avenue
Chatswood
NSW 2067
Tel: 612 941 78572
Fax: 612 941 77617
email: janetr@janetsart.com.au
website: www.janetsart. com.au

Handwork Supplies*
212 Commercial Road
South Yarra
Victoria 3141
Tel: 613 982 08399
Fax: 613 982 08312
email: handwork@ozemail.com.au
website: www.handworks.com.au

NEW ZEALAND

General
Gordon Harris Ltd*
4 Gillies Avenue
New Market
Auckland
Tel: 09 520 4466
Fax: 09 524 0391

Little Johns
170 Victoria Street
Wellington
Tel: 385 2099
Fax: 385 2090
email:littlejohns@xtra.co.nz

FURTHER READING

Baldwin, Peter, **Toy Theatres of the World**, A. Zwemmer Ltd

Brommer, Gerald, **Collage Techniques**, Watson Guptill

Jackson, Paul, **Paper Pop-Ups**, Rockport Publishers

Johnson, Cathy, **Watercolour Tricks and Techniques**, Northlight Books

La Ferla, Jane, **Gilding: Easy Techniques and Elegant Projects with Metal Leaf**, Cassell

Shannon, Faith, **The Art and Craft of Paper**, Mitchell Beazley

Stevens, Clive, **Papercraft School**, Readers Digest

Stoker, Andrew and Williamson, Sasha, **Fantastic Folds**, G. Weidenfeld & Nicolson

Swinton, David, **The Magic of Paper Sculpture**, Cassell

Wagstaff, Liz, **The Gilding Book**, Lorenz Books

ACKNOWLEDGEMENTS

My heartfelt thanks go to all of the following:

Mark – my driving force, confidant and companion, and without whom this project would have been impossible.

Elizabeth Inman – for her understanding and support, and for having the vision and confidence to allow my imagination to run free.

Cath Laing and Andy Charman – for their expert editorial guidance and advice.

Zul Mukhida – for the beautiful photographs, and three delightful days in his studio, watching a master at work.

Gigi Sandberg – for her energy-giving support and endless enthusiasm.

Josie and Marc – for all the tea and apple cake.

Mum and Dad – for that beautiful puppet theatre and all those wonderful Christmas memories.

Mariëtte Brinkman and Maarten Endt, Menno and Matthijs – for their support and friendship throughout my four years in Amsterdam.

Jon Barratt for thirty years of friendship and laughter.

Joyce, Fred, Vanessa, Mark and Joel for all their love and support.

About the Author

Robert Burgess has been designing and making toy theatres for many years. Initially they were 'one off' projects for family and friends, which then led to commissions for special occasions. Robert then decided to use the experience he had gained to create a range of miniature theatres. They range in size from the tiniest 'theatre in a matchbox', to the biggest and most sumptuous Victorian-style theatres. Robert specialized in packaging at university, so it is no surprise that the boxes accompanying the theatres play an important part in the design.

Robert's theatres sell to enthusiasts from all over the world. His theatres are featured in the Jim Henson Foundation exhibition and the Great Small Works exhibition in New York in the Autumn of 2000.

Now living in Brighton, Robert makes and sells bespoke toy theatres. Each theatre in the range is one of a limited edition and a certificate accompanies the theatre to verify this. This means that no two theatres are exactly alike.

Robert's current projects include a children's book and a theatre kit inspired by the Royal Pavilion in Brighton. He is also in the process of developing a collector's set of theatres and opera houses from around the world.

Robert also organizes numerous toy theatre workshops for children and adults alike; these have proved to be extremely successful.

Robert Burgess has a website you can visit, www.papertheatre.freeserve.co.uk, his email address is rob@papertheatre.freeserve.co.uk

INDEX

TITLES AVAILABLE FROM
GMC Publications
BOOKS

WOODWORKING

40 More Woodworking Plans & Projects	*GMC Publications*	Pine Furniture Projects for the Home	*Dave Mackenzie*
Bird Boxes and Feeders for the Garden	*Dave Mackenzie*	Router Magic: Jigs, Fixtures and Tricks to	
Complete Woodfinishing	*Ian Hosker*	Unleash your Router's Full Potential	*Bill Hylton*
David Charlesworth's Furniture-Making Techniques	*David Charlesworth*	Routing for Beginners	*Anthony Bailey*
Electric Woodwork	*Jeremy Broun*	The Scrollsaw: Twenty Projects	*John Everett*
Furniture & Cabinetmaking Projects	*GMC Publications*	Sharpening Pocket Reference Book	*Jim Kingshott*
Furniture Projects	*Rod Wales*	Sharpening: The Complete Guide	*Jim Kingshott*
Furniture Restoration (Practical Crafts)	*Kevin Jan Bonner*	Space-Saving Furniture Projects	*Dave Mackenzie*
Furniture Restoration and Repair for Beginners	*Kevin Jan Bonner*	Stickmaking: A Complete Course	*Andrew Jones & Clive George*
Furniture Restoration Workshop	*Kevin Jan Bonner*	Stickmaking Handbook	*Andrew Jones & Clive George*
Green Woodwork	*Mike Abbott*	Test Reports: *The Router* and	
The Incredible Router	*Jeremy Broun*	*Furniture & Cabinetmaking*	*GMC Publications*
Making & Modifying Woodworking Tools	*Jim Kingshott*	Veneering: A Complete Course	*Ian Hosker*
Making Chairs and Tables	*GMC Publications*	Woodfinishing Handbook (Practical Crafts)	*Ian Hosker*
Making Fine Furniture	*Tom Darby*	Woodworking Plans and Projects	*GMC Publications*
Making Little Boxes from Wood	*John Bennett*	Woodworking with the Router: Professional	
Making Shaker Furniture	*Barry Jackson*	Router Techniques any Woodworker can Use	*Bill Hylton & Fred Matlack*
Making Woodwork Aids and Devices	*Robert Wearing*	The Workshop	*Jim Kingshott*

WOODTURNING

Adventures in Woodturning	*David Springett*	Practical Tips for Woodturners	*GMC Publications*
Bert Marsh: Woodturner	*Bert Marsh*	Spindle Turning	*GMC Publications*
Bill Jones' Notes from the Turning Shop	*Bill Jones*	Turning Miniatures in Wood	*John Sainsbury*
Bill Jones' Further Notes from the Turning Shop	*Bill Jones*	Turning Wooden Toys	*Terry Lawrence*
Colouring Techniques for Woodturners	*Jan Sanders*	Understanding Woodturning	*Ann & Bob Phillips*
The Craftsman Woodturner	*Peter Child*	Useful Techniques for Woodturners	*GMC Publications*
Decorative Techniques for Woodturners	*Hilary Bowen*	Useful Woodturning Projects	*GMC Publications*
Essential Tips for Woodturners	*GMC Publications*	Woodturning: Bowls, Platters, Hollow Forms, Vases,	
Faceplate Turning	*GMC Publications*	Vessels, Bottles, Flasks, Tankards, Plates	*GMC Publications*
Fun at the Lathe	*R.C. Bell*	Woodturning: A Foundation Course (New Edition)	*Keith Rowley*
Illustrated Woodturning Techniques	*John Hunnex*	Woodturning: A Source Book of Shapes	*John Hunnex*
Intermediate Woodturning Projects	*GMC Publications*	Woodturning Jewellery	*Hilary Bowen*
Keith Rowley's Woodturning Projects	*Keith Rowley*	Woodturning Masterclass	*Tony Boase*
Make Money from Woodturning	*Ann & Bob Phillips*	Woodturning Techniques	*GMC Publications*
Multi-Centre Woodturning	*Ray Hopper*	*Woodturning* Tools & Equipment Test Reports	*GMC Publications*
Pleasure and Profit from Woodturning	*Reg Sherwin*	Woodturning Wizardry	*David Springett*
Practical Tips for Turners & Carvers	*GMC Publications*		

WOODCARVING

The Art of the Woodcarver	*GMC Publications*	Understanding Woodcarving	*GMC Publications*
Carving Birds & Beasts	*GMC Publications*	Understanding Woodcarving in the Round	*GMC Publications*
Carving on Turning	*Chris Pye*	Useful Techniques for Woodcarvers	*GMC Publications*
Carving Realistic Birds	*David Tippey*	Wildfowl Carving – Volume 1	*Jim Pearce*
Decorative Woodcarving	*Jeremy Williams*	Wildfowl Carving – Volume 2	*Jim Pearce*
Essential Tips for Woodcarvers	*GMC Publications*	The Woodcarvers	*GMC Publications*
Essential Woodcarving Techniques	*Dick Onians*	Woodcarving: A Complete Course	*Ron Butterfield*
Lettercarving in Wood: A Practical Course	*Chris Pye*	Woodcarving: A Foundation Course	*Zoë Gertner*
Power Tools for Woodcarving	*David Tippey*	Woodcarving for Beginners	*GMC Publications*
Practical Tips for Turners & Carvers	*GMC Publications*	*Woodcarving* Tools & Equipment Test Reports	*GMC Publications*
Relief Carving in Wood: A Practical Introduction	*Chris Pye*	Woodcarving Tools, Materials & Equipment	*Chris Pye*

UPHOLSTERY

Seat Weaving (Practical Crafts)	*Ricky Holdstock*	Upholstery Restoration	*David James*
The Upholsterer's Pocket Reference Book	*David James*	Upholstery Techniques & Projects	*David James*
Upholstery: A Complete Course (Revised Edition)	*David James*		

TOYMAKING

Designing & Making Wooden Toys	*Terry Kelly*	Restoring Rocking Horses	*Clive Green & Anthony Dew*
Fun to Make Wooden Toys & Games	*Jeff & Jennie Loader*	Scrollsaw Toy Projects	*Ivor Carlyle*
Making Board, Peg & Dice Games	*Jeff & Jennie Loader*	Wooden Toy Projects	*GMC Publications*
Making Wooden Toys & Games	*Jeff & Jennie Loader*		

DOLLS' HOUSES AND MINIATURES

Architecture for Dolls' Houses	*Joyce Percival*	Making Miniature Gardens	*Freida Gray*
Beginners' Guide to the Dolls' House Hobby	*Jean Nisbett*	Making Miniature Oriental Rugs & Carpets	*Meik & Ian McNaughton*
The Complete Dolls' House Book	*Jean Nisbett*	Making Period Dolls' House Accessories	*Andrea Barham*
The Dolls' House 1/24 Scale: A Complete Introduction	*Jean Nisbett*	Making Period Dolls' House Furniture	*Derek & Sheila Rowbottom*
Dolls' House Accessories, Fixtures and Fittings	*Andrea Barham*	Making Tudor Dolls' Houses	*Derek Rowbottom*
Dolls' House Bathrooms: Lots of Little Loos	*Patricia King*	Making Unusual Miniatures	*Graham Spalding*
Dolls' House Fireplaces and Stoves	*Patricia King*	Making Victorian Dolls' House Furniture	*Patricia King*
Easy to Make Dolls' House Accessories	*Andrea Barham*	Miniature Bobbin Lace	*Roz Snowden*
Heraldic Miniature Knights	*Peter Greenhill*	Miniature Embroidery for the Victorian Dolls' House	*Pamela Warner*
Make Your Own Dolls' House Furniture	*Maurice Harper*	Miniature Needlepoint Carpets	*Janet Granger*
Making Dolls' House Furniture	*Patricia King*	The Secrets of the Dolls' House Makers	*Jean Nisbett*
Making Georgian Dolls' Houses	*Derek Rowbottom*		

CRAFTS

American Patchwork Designs in Needlepoint	*Melanie Tacon*	An Introduction to Crewel Embroidery	*Mave Glenny*
A Beginners' Guide to Rubber Stamping	*Brenda Hunt*	Making Character Bears	*Valerie Tyler*
Celtic Knotwork Designs	*Sheila Sturrock*	Making Greetings Cards for Beginners	*Pat Sutherland*
Celtic Knotwork Handbook	*Sheila Sturrock*	Making Hand-Sewn Boxes: Techniques and Projects	*Jackie Woolsey*
Collage from Seeds, Leaves and Flowers	*Joan Carver*	Making Knitwear Fit	*Pat Ashforth & Steve Plummer*
Complete Pyrography	*Stephen Poole*	Needlepoint: A Foundation Course	*Sandra Hardy*
Creating Knitwear Designs	*Pat Ashforth & Steve Plummer*	Pyrography Designs	*Norma Gregory*
Creative Doughcraft	*Patrica Hughes*	Pyrography Handbook (Practical Crafts)	*Stephen Pool*
Creative Embroidery Techniques		Ribbons and Roses	*Lee Lockhead*
Using Colour Through Gold	*Daphne J. Ashby & Jackie Woolsey*	Tassel Making for Beginners	*Enid Taylor*
Cross Stitch Kitchen Projects	*Janet Granger*	Tatting Collage	*Lindsay Rogers*
Cross Stitch on Colour	*Sheena Rogers*	Temari: A Traditional Japanese Embroidery Technique	*Margaret Ludlow*
Designing and Making Cards	*Glennis Gilruth*	Theatre Models in Paper and Card	*Robert Burgess*
Embroidery Tips & Hints	*Harold Hayes*	Wool Embroidery and Design	*Lee Lockhead*

HOME & GARDEN

Home Ownership: Buying and Maintaining	*Nicholas Snelling*	Security for the Householder: Fitting Locks	*E. Phillips*
The Living Tropical Greenhouse	*John and Maureen Tampion*	and Other Devices	

VIDEOS

Drop-in and Pinstuffed Seats	*David James*	Twists and Advanced Turning	*Dennis White*
Stuffover Upholstery	*David James*	Sharpening the Professional Way	*Jim Kingshott*
Elliptical Turning	*David Springett*	Sharpening Turning & Carving Tools	*Jim Kingshott*
Woodturning Wizardry	*David Springett*	Bowl Turning	*John Jordan*
Turning Between Centres: The Basics	*Dennis White*	Hollow Turning	*John Jordan*
Turning Bowls	*Dennis White*	Woodturning: A Foundation Course	*Keith Rowley*
Boxes, Goblets and Screw Threads	*Dennis White*	Carving a Figure: The Female Form	*Ray Gonzalez*
Novelties and Projects	*Dennis White*	The Router: A Beginner's Guide	*Alan Goodsell*
Classic Profiles	*Dennis White*	The Scroll Saw: A Beginner's Guide	*John Burke*

MAGAZINES

WOODTURNING ◆ WOODCARVING ◆ FURNITURE & CABINETMAKING
THE DOLLS' HOUSE MAGAZINE ◆ CREATIVE CRAFTS FOR THE HOME
THE ROUTER ◆ THE SCROLLSAW ◆ BUSINESSMATTERS

◆

The above represents a full list of all titles currently published or scheduled to be published.
All are available direct from the Publishers or through bookshops, newsagents and specialist retailers.
To place an order, or to obtain a complete catalogue, contact:

GMC Publications,
Castle Place, 166 High Street, Lewes, East Sussex BN7 1XU, United Kingdom
Tel: 01273 488005 Fax: 01273 478606

Orders by credit card are accepted